The One and the Many

Nicholas Hagger is a philosopher, cultural historian, poet and former lecturer in the Middle East and Japan. He is also a prolific author whose long-term project is to present the universe, world history and human life in terms of the mystic Fire or Light, the metaphysical vision that is central to his work.

By the same author

The Fire and the Stones
Selected Poems
The Universe and the Light
Awakening to the Light
A Mystic Way
A White Radiance
A Spade Fresh With Mud
A Smell of Leaves and Summer
The Warlords
Overlord

The One and the Many

Universalism and the Vision of Unity

NICHOLAS HAGGER

ELEMENT
Shaftesbury, Dorset • Boston, Massachusetts • Melbourne, Victoria

© Element Books Limited 1999
Text © Nicholas Hagger 1999

First published in the UK in 1999 by
Element Books Limited
Shaftesbury, Dorset SP7 8BP

Published in the USA in 1999 by
Element Books, Inc
160 North Washington Street, Boston MA 02114

Published in Australia in 1999 by
Element Books
and distributed by Penguin Australia Limited
487 Maroondah Highway, Ringwood, Victoria 3134

Cover design by Mark Slader
Design and Illustration by Alison Goldsmith
Typeset by Wendy Murdoch
Printed and bound in Great Britain by
Creative Print and Design, Ebbw Vale, Wales

British Library Cataloguing in Publication
data available
Library of Congress Cataloging in Publication
data available

ISBN 1 86204 532 1

CONTENTS

'One and Many in Pre-Socratic Philosophy.'
Title of a book

'The One remains, the many change and pass;
Heaven's light forever shines, Earth's shadows fly;
Life, like a dome of many-coloured glass,
Stains the white radiance of Eternity,
Until Death tramples it to fragments....
That Light whose smile kindles the Universe,
That Beauty in which all things work and move....'

Shelley, *Adonais*

'I would make a pilgrimage to the deserts of Arabia to find
the man who could make me understand how the *one can
be many*.'

Coleridge

PREFACE

At the beginning of the 20th century a second scientific revolution was set in motion with Einstein's relativity theory and the discovery of quantum mechanics. This new physics influenced the philosophy of the day, and found its way into the work of Bergson (the philosopher of Vitalism), Whitehead, Husserl, T E Hulme and others. In the metaphysical tradition of Plato, Leibniz and Kant, they attempted to create models of reality by which every element of our experience could be interpreted. After 1910 this process was curtailed by the ascendancy of the Vienna Circle whose logical positivism and linguistic analysis insisted that metaphysical principles must be verified. I have endeavoured to retrieve the Vitalist tradition and return to the source of Western philosophy, to its Pre-Socratic origins: Heracleitus's Fire and (Vitalist) flux, and Parmenides' One.

The vision of the One has inspired all the deepest philosophers, poets and mystics in all cultures. According to this vision the Universe is fundamentally One not only in terms of spatial area – it is a Whole, the aggregate of its parts, just as a forest is the aggregate of all the individual trees within it – but also in terms of its originating principle. According to the vision, the Universe originated in and emerged from one seed, Dante's 'infinitesimal point', the 'singularity' of modern cosmologists. Whereas the holistic view of the Whole's spatial 'area' is often as materialistic as the opposite, reductionist view of its parts, the view of an 'origin' beyond physics is only metaphysical. All the multiplicity, the manifold phenomena within Nature and the cosmos, the many, originated in and emerged from the One which is beyond physics and whose manifest ingredient and texture it shares.

According to the vision, this One principle is the Fire or Light, the metaphysical principle which permeates the Universe it produced and which can be known within as Inner Light in the experience of illumination. This One principle has inspired the stone temples of past tradition, much of which is buried under the materialistic brambles and undergrowth of recent times. It is best approached through present experience, for which there is no substitute. The focus for philosophers, poets and mystics must therefore be on the metaphysical Universe in which they operate, and which needs to be described. Such a description requires a Metaphysical Revolution in philosophy to scythe away 85 years of humanism, scepticism and materialism that have obscured an approach to the One just as jungle and low cloud obscure the peak of a high mountain and the sun. The purpose of the Metaphysical Revolution is to clear the jungle so that what is – both above and below – can be truly seen. Part 1 of this book begins on this process.

A new metaphysical philosophy is needed, and to this end I have been developing Universalism throughout the 1990s. My philosophy of Universalism sees and describes the Universe as a Whole which has originated in the One metaphysical principle of the Fire or Light. Universalism starts with the premise of Oneness and explores the consequences of Oneness in all disciplines – most notably in physics, history, philosophy and literature. Each attempt to define Universalism is like an expedition into the jungle round Angkor Wat in Cambodia, and each attempt brings back more information about the stones beneath the tree-roots, some damaged by iconoclastic occupiers, rationalistic, materialistic Khmer Rouges. A new metaphysical philosophy has to be hewn out of the jungle of humanism, scepticism and materialism before a cleared view can be presented to the world, a coherent, self-consistent and symmetrical philosophy like the main temple at Angkor Wat standing in a clearing open to the sun. Part 2 of this book represents further probes and further clearing of the ground in preparation for a full revelation of the new philosophy.

A metaphysical approach has a huge effect on civilization and culture. Cultures deprived of metaphysical sap are like gardens of brittle, etiolated trees and flowers. Our culture is one-dimensional – materialistic – and following the deaths of Eliot, Jung and Toynbee has almost entirely lost contact with its metaphysical roots, its origin. The waste land has extended. My mission is to redeem the waste land, and the vision of the metaphysical Fire or Light can do this by bringing about a Revolution in philosophy and culture and starting a new mystical direction in poetry and literature. At a time when a world government is looming and all cultures are drawing together into one globalist civilization, it is important that a coming common culture should be 'origin'-based (based on the metaphysical One Fire or Light, which is common to all cultures) rather than spatial 'area'-based (based on a shallow one-dimensional, materialistic multi-culturalism that has no rootedness and merely weakens each regional culture's traditional energy). In short, the coming common culture should be Fire-based rather than money-based. Part 3 of this work makes a start on redeeming the waste land of our culture by clearing it like a dynamic gardener tackling the back-breaking task of creating order and symmetry where Nature, out of control, has left a jungle.

The aim of this book is to leave the reader with an understanding of the metaphysical Universe in which he or she lives; of the need for physics, philosophy, history and literature to describe it accurately; and of the importance of transforming our arid, humanistic, sceptical, materialistic culture in which souls too readily wither and atrophy. In short, I call for a Revolution in all disciplines to hew a track through the jungle of multiplicity towards the life-saving One.

August 1998

PART ONE

THE METAPHYSICAL UNIVERSE

REVOLUTION: RECLAIMING THE PALACE OF METAPHYSICS

I sometimes dream that the scientific and philosophical Establishment is a great country house as large as Buckingham Palace or Windsor Castle with a magnificent lawn and a notice saying 'Trespassers will be prosecuted'. (In fact reality is more urban: the Royal Society of Newton is now in Carlton House Terrace, London and the Royal Institute of Philosophy is in Gordon Square, where Russell gave his lectures on logical atomism in 1916.) 'This great house used to be ours,' I told a group of pro-metaphysical philosophers, 'and between 1840 and 1920 we were gradually expelled by upstart scientific and philosophical reductionists. It's time to go through the hole in the hedge and stand on the lawn and reclaim our birthright.'

Metaphysics is the sumptuous, palatial science of a universal Whole or All and refers to *all* possible concepts – not merely existing concepts – including infinity and the entire Universe. Majestically, it includes all things abstract or concrete, natural or supernatural, known or unknown, probable or improbable, the sensible and the supersensible. It includes cosmology, epistemology, spiritual psychology, and ontology, and offers a system of general ideas in terms of which every element of our experience can be interpreted. It includes the spiritual and divine Traditions as well as the mind and body – four levels.

Since 1840 materialism has disqualified all energy that cannot be verified by sense data. Scientific reductionists have reduced the Universe and men to an accidental collection of granular atoms, cells and neurons, and all mental events to physical events. Philosophical reductionists have reduced all statements to collections of words whose ideas must be verifiable to have meaning. Inner mystical experience is deemed unverifiable and therefore meaningless. Man has been dehumanized.

Until recently there has been a prevailing scepticism, and the materialists still feel in a strong position. At a symposium on the primacy of reductionism in the natural sciences, held at Cambridge in August 1992, they were in a majority of over 80 per cent. There is nothing hidden behind the Universe, they argue; what you see is what you get. Cosmologists like Stephen Hawking assume that the Universe can be fully explained by observation, sense data and mathematics, which will show that the four forces of physics are unified. (The date for this demonstration has been put back to 2010.) Neo-Darwinist biologists like Dawkins show that evolution is a chance activity. Deconstructionist philosophers like Derrida exclude the spiritual. Man is living, in P W Atkins' phrase, on a 'dunghill of purposeless interconnected corruption' in which everything is 'bleak' and 'barren' – like a Beckett character.

But where is the evidence for scepticism? Materialists, as Whitehead pointed out in *Process and Reality* (2.2.5), believe that atoms endure, whereas modern particle colliders, applying the tenets of quantum physics, show that atoms can disappear back into the quantum vacuum from which they manifested as one of a pair of 'virtual particles'. Neo-Darwinists now distinguish variation that cannot be inherited from variation that can, but no one has found a part-human, part-ape skull. Where is the evidence that we emerged from the ape? It does not exist, it is an assumption – a belief. The sceptical Derrida pronounces there is no hidden reality in the soul or the Universe – *il n'y a rien hors du texte* – but where is his evidence for this view, which conflicts with the religious and paranormal experience of millions?

All of a sudden, people are questioning philosophical scepticism, doubting the doubters, echoing Hamlet's 'There are more things in heaven and earth, Horatio,/Than are dreamt of in your philosophy'. Following relativity and quantum theory, no longer can the scientist be a separated and detached observer of the Universe he is describing; rather he is indivisibly connected to it and part of it. And no longer can he exclude all that cannot be explained by his sceptical reason. In the quantum, non-local, whole Universe, there is a place for intuition.

There is a feeling that metaphysics was wrongly debunked by logical positivists who focused on the material, rational, social ego and its logical, analytical powers and ignored the intuitive part of man that Bergson, William James, T E Hulme, Whitehead, and Husserl were all interested in around 1910. On 24 March 1993 the entire Late Show on BBC2 was devoted to a discussion of why British philosophy has failed to be known for exploring the Universe and Christopher Peacock, Professor of Metaphysical Philosophy at Oxford, spoke at some length. People are now actually sitting up and paying attention to the metaphysical view.

Scepticism is a by-product of Rationalism, which emphasizes a partial quality of the human being. There is now a feeling growing that the whole of man includes his soul and spirit, which are indivisibly connected to the Universe; that science should accept as evidence the consensus of what mystics report about their inner experience; and that it is time to restore metaphysics and effect the 'much-desired union of science and metaphysics' which Bergson called for in 1903. There is no time to wait for a gradual change – there has been too long a wait already. A sudden and abrupt change is the only way.

The Metaphysical Revolution (or Counter-Revolution) challenges post-1840 reductionism in science and post-1910 reductionism in philosophy, and lets back into science and philosophy what has been wrongly excluded. It connects science and philosophy to a new view of the Universe: that it is a Whole with a hidden energy behind it, the force that counterbalances gravity which Newton saw as light and Einstein as a constant with 'hidden variables'.

This hidden energy is associated with the well-documented experience of illumination, which mystics have known since the beginning of recorded history and which St Augustine, Pope Gregory the Great, St Bernard and St John of the Cross, among many, have all regarded as God. In *The Fire and the Stones* I state the 5,000-year-old Tradition of this experience of the Fire or Light; I begin with Pascal, whose experience of Fire on Monday 23 November 1654 made such an impact on him that he sewed his written account of it into his doublet and wore it for the last eight years of his life.

My Form from Movement theory (which is stated in full at the end of *The Universe and the Light*) traces the origin and birth of the Universe from the first principle of an infinite and moving metaphysical Fire or Light – compare Heracleitus's Fire – which manifests into creation and evolution. This Light is behind cosmology and permeates Nature as a hidden reality that has flowed into the phenomenal world: we are like sponges in a sea of Light we can see during meditation. The Light is central to history as it is the founding principle of civilizations, which, as I showed in *The Fire and the Stones*, begin when a mystic such as Mohammed has a vision of the divine Fire or Light. Out of this mystical vision a religion develops which inspires the growth of a civilization and empire. The civilization declines when the vision wanes and is no longer renewed.

The Metaphysical Revolution unifies all disciplines in relation to the Fire or Light: metaphysics, mysticism, world history, religion, physics, biology, psychology, philosophy and of course the arts. This new metaphysical principle of the Fire or Light can be *experienced* existentially, as we see from the mystics. I have sought to make metaphysics existential as well as a forum for rational speculation about all possible concepts.

At the personal level, the Metaphysical Revolution encourages a practical experience of the divine Light and advocates a Mystic Revival. At a more theoretical level, it seeks to redefine university syllabuses to liberate the young from the dominance of scepticism and materialism. At the universal level it promotes a new philosophy of Universalism, which has replaced Existentialism as an 'existenzphilosophie'. Universalism asserts that the universal energy of the Light manifests into the Universe and guides our soul or universal being with great universality. It is an experience which is the essence of all religions, and so can be received both outside or within any religion.

A true Theory of Everything is possible if we make sense of all levels of what is known, including the spiritual and divine, in terms of the Fire or Light. Materialist cosmologists speak of a Theory of Everything that will unite the four known forces of physics, but were they to find this it would not explain conversation, love and the noblest human feelings. Theirs is a partial Theory of Everything which includes only those concepts that are known to the five senses.

My call to the revolutionary barricades need not end like the uprising in *Les Misérables*. There may be a negotiation and metaphysics may be offered a wing in the great house – or may even drive out the reductionists, like Mr Toad returning to Toad Hall and triumphantly driving out the upstart stoats and weasels.

LIVING IN A UNIVERSE OF FIRE

As I sit looking out to sea in Cornwall, the light often dances on the surface of the water and in the curl of each gentle wave. Tens of thousands of points of light flash out and fade each split second, to be replaced by new points in new spaces. Twice in my poems I have tried to catch the elation I feel at thrilling to such an alive Universe:

'The jumping of exploding diamonds and the
    sparkle of crystal,
I flashed jubilation like a white hot mirror'
                                    ('The Silence', 1965-6)

and

'The light leaps off your Worthing sea
Like shoals of leaping mackerel'
                                    ('Flow: Moon and Sea', 1971)

But, gazing at the jumping lights right out to the horizon, I see the surface of the water as an image for the quantum vacuum and the pouring of particles into existence. According to the work of Edgard Gunzig and others, pairs of virtual particles manifest from nothing into something, live a split second and die back into the void, unless they combine with energy and become real, enduring particles. Everything that is has come out of Nothingness and exists as a perpetual dance of light.

I present the Universe in terms of a manifesting infinite Fire which is experienced within as Light. I propose that this Fire – the Fire of Heracleitus – was an infinite self-aware, *moving* first principle, a Nothingness. (No one, except possibly Heracleitus, has ever started with a *moving* first principle.) A limitation in movement formed a spiral, a more limited and undefined Non-Being, and out of the interplay between the two and the pressure of the movement on the spiral two pre-particles arose. One of these was annihilated and the other received energy from the pressure and became an empty point or pre-vacuum, a more defined Non-Being. The point spread and expanded, evolving more structure, and became Being – the quantum vacuum. The infinite movement of Nothingness continued to give energy to Being so that virtual particles emerged from the quantum vacuum in pairs and, receiving energy, one particle in each pair became a real particle and endured. Form arose like dancing, exploding points of light on a Cornish sea.

In my account of creation, my Form from Movement Theory, I describe how real particles became galaxies by inflation – how tiny points of light became stars – and organisms emerged and ascended into hierarchical wholes from one organism. Cosmology and evolution can therefore be seen as manifesting from an organizing force of Fire that is beyond Nature. This force was the expanding force of Light that Newton sought, Einstein's cosmological constant and Bohm's hidden variability. In the same way energy which manifests from the organizing force stimulates and drives the neurons of the brain. Consciousness thus flows into the brain and directs brain activity. Mind is not brain-function as the materialists assert. I hold that mystics are able to see this infinite Fire – in *The Fire and the Stones* I give hundreds of experiences drawn from the cultures of the last 5,000 years – and that the vision of the Fire is the central idea of 25 civilizations (and therefore of world history).

Nature is thus an organic, living *energy* which evolves to higher and higher hierarchical wholes. My view differs from that of many holists because I see Nature as manifesting from an infinite principle, the Fire, which pre-existed Nature and is beyond it. To go back to my opening analogy, forms emerged like points of light from the sea of Fire or Being, into which they return.

We are thus an inextricable part of a Universe of energy. The energy of the Fire manifests into the Universe, pours into us and guides our universal being (or soul or spirit), filling us with infused knowledge and wisdom. We live in a sea of Fire which has marvellous properties of healing and wisdom, and at every level we are healthiest when we admit the Fire.

Mystics have seen it as 'white Light' in every Age. They close their eyes and wait, and the Fire eventually appears as Light behind their closed eyes on the inner 'screen' viewed by the 'third eye' or eye of contemplation. At first it seems watery, then it is like fire, then it is like dawn breaking and finally it is a dazzling sun, sometimes so bright that it is hard to look at it. It is possible to wait for it for an hour and a half before it first appears, and many who meditate for only half an hour finish their meditation without reaching the starting-point. The Fire is God according to the Christian Tradition of St Augustine, St Gregory and St Bernard (while God is the darkness within or behind the Fire according to an Eastern Tradition of Dionysius the Areopagite). Yet many religious people have not seen it and do not expect to see it, including many monks and nuns who pray with words and do not *gaze* within. Even Quakers, who profess 'the Inward Light', sometimes fill the silence with words and confess they have never seen the Fire.

We can understand what happens when we open to the energy around us if we consider metaphysics. 'Metaphysics' has two meanings. It is first and foremost a branch of traditional philosophy, and as such encompasses ontology (the study of Being or Reality, i.e. the Fire), transpersonal psychology (the part of the self – the universal being – which relates to Being or the Fire at its deepest level), epistemology (what can be known about Being or the Fire) and cosmology (the structure of the Universe). Metaphysics also means (especially in the USA) the 'supersensible', what is beyond the five senses. I use the term in both meanings. As the metaphysical whole perspective was wrongly debunked in the early 20th century I have launched a Metaphysical Revolution to restore the metaphysical Universe of the Fire in contemporary thought and reflect it in university syllabuses, so that the younger generation can contact true values during their studies.

The soul is the bridge between our eternal spirit and perishable psychological mind, and when the Fire licks into our spirit and soul or universal being, we are refreshed and open to pure energy. As our souls are healed and nourished by Fire we are aware of new powers of understanding. When the Fire burns through into our mind, psychological problems are instantly put right. Jung said in his commentary to *The Secret of the Golden Flower* that the Light (i.e. the 'Golden Flower', for in the Chinese 'Kuang', 'Light', is hidden between the two characters 'Golden Flower') 'brings about a solution of psychic complexities, and thereby frees the inner personality from emotional and intellectual entanglements, creating thus a unity of being'. There is an immediate effect on behaviour, and abruptly people give up smoking, stop drinking and cease to be promiscuous, as a natural yearning for purification cleanses their senses. They become naturally good, and do not mug others, steal cars, abuse children, or do any of the terrible things we read about every day in our newspapers. At the physical level the Fire brings healing for we are, in both body and mind, systems of light, and the Fire manifests into an energy of very high frequency beyond the gamma end of the electromagnetic spectrum, and its energy heals our energy systems.

The Fire only enters the soul when one has bypassed the rational, social ego (the main obstacle to enlightenment for Zen Buddhists, who bypass it by silence and 'mind-blowing' koans). This bypassing is the main purpose of the Mystic Way. First there is an awakening, then a purgation of the ego and of its attachment to the world of the senses and their desires (the Dark Night of Sense). Illumination by the Fire, which is experienced as Light, happens when the soul or universal being is suitably detached from its sensual ego. After raptures and an increase in contemplation the mystic is plunged back into darkness (the Dark Night of the Spirit) where there is a further purging of the spirit and a further detachment from sensual appetites. Finally the mystic emerges into the unitive life. He or she now has unity of being and perceives the Universe as a unity.

In this unitive phase, the contact between the Fire and the soul is daily and effortless. In this phase, if one sits quietly with closed eyes and breathes deeply within a minute or two the Fire appears behind the closed eyes, seen with the eye of contemplation (a subtle organ as opposed to the bodily eye of the flesh and the mind's eye of reason). There will be surges of energy from the beyond which pour down the back, tingling the spine and making the flesh go goose-pimply. These surges pass through the thighs and out through the feet. To open to the Fire is to let it pour in 'from the top down', an opposite movement from the yogic 'bottom-up', when the movement is from the bottom chakras up to the top.

Conversely, one can sit and let the energy flow in and rotate round the energy body. One can then beam it out, perhaps with outstretched hands, send it across vast distances in the form of prayer or absent healing. Wordless, contemplative prayer in which the Fire is sent out afar works – a study in the US has shown that patients in a hospital who were the unknowing objects of prayer all got better, whereas those not prayed for did not. Radionics practitioners are sure that absent healing works.

The Universe of Fire is not an élitist notion which merely applies to the illumined, to the few who have found their way. Everyone in humankind has brotherhood (or sisterhood) in the Fire, whether they know it or not, and those who have achieved unity of being know within that they are responsible for all humankind. I want to be completely clear on this very important point. All living creatures live and move within the Universe of Fire, and those who realise this and consciously admit the Fire into their own living enjoy 'the peace that passeth understanding', ocean-like reservoirs of energy, insight and creativity, and a sense of meaning, purpose and direction aided by Providential 'luck' that those who are not aware of it do not enjoy. The illumined lead forward and further raise the heightened consciousness of humankind, and no matter how unexalted or lowly their social position they leave behind great works and deeds which inspire and encourage the unillumined by their example. Mystics, thinkers and saints such as William Blake, Matthew Arnold and Mother Teresa never aspired to be Presidents or Prime Ministers, but the example they set in their collected works or deeds as poets, painters, educators or carers has been or will be transmitted to future generations as a legacy that helps to raise the level of humankind's awareness and consciousness of itself.

The illumined have a duty to help the poor. Transcendence works in the world through the illumined as it did through Mother Teresa, who embodied God's love as she helped the poor. The illumined feel moved – guided – to serve others and to seek posts of responsibility where they can make things better for other people. They found new institutions and conduct reforms. The ultimate aim of the illumined is to form a world government that will abolish injustice and inequality and bring peace. The illumined tread in the footsteps of Plato (who saw existence as shadows thrown from a fire onto a cave wall) and attempt to create their own 'republic': an ideal world government run by illumined, compassionate elders who make things better for the unillumined at every level, redistributing food, abolishing local wars and setting an example of gentleness in their dealings with all men. The illumined attempt to practise enlightened amelioration.

A concern with the souls of all humankind is Universalist. There has been religious Universalism (the belief that all humankind is saved, not just Christians) and historical Universalism (the study of world history). There is now the possibility of political Universalism (the belief that there should be human rights for all humankind, regardless of race or creed). If there is a New World Order around AD 2000 ostensibly under the United Nations, as many wish, then political Universalism can become a reality in our time. The illumined mystic who perceives the unity of the Universe regards all humankind as his brother or sister, and with humanitarian compassion actively works to improve its lot.

Such a selfless and ameliorist social outlook is implicit in my philosophy of Universalism, the successor to Existentialism as an 'existenzphilosophie', which holds that the universal energy of the

Fire burns into the universal being from the Universe, giving a unitive vision, and that all illumined people feel a duty to help the poor and make things better for their fellow human beings, wherever they find them; in their own small locality for some, or from a national or international platform or conference chamber in the case of world leaders. Meliorism is a natural consequence of personal illumination. The illumined colour their culture with their illumined works and transmit their vision to the unillumined, who make efforts to replicate and reflect the vision of 'natural goodness' and work for the amelioration of humankind.

To open to and experience influxes of the universal energy of the Fire is to live in perfect harmony and balance with Nature – in perfect balance between Yin and Yang as the Chinese put it. The mind, soul and spirit are in perfect balance, and all the faculties perfectly complement each other: the instinctive, emotional, rational and intellectual faculties (the *intellectus* or intellect is a faculty of higher perception as it is in Shelley's 'Hymn to Intellectual Beauty', and is quite separate from the reason). Right brain and left brain are in perfect balance and harmony, as are knowledge of the infinite and one's sense of social being. Unitive or Universalist poems show the infinite in specific social settings.

To open to the universal energy is to experience the common essence of all religion. The Fire, which is experienced as the Light, is what all the religions have in common: it is the Quaker Inner Light, the Christian Divine Light (of Christ, the Light of the World), the Orthodox Transfiguration, Islamic Sufi fana, Hindu samadhi, Tantric Hinduism's kundalini, Mahayana Buddhist enlightenment, the Tibetan Buddhist Clear Light of the Void, the Taoist Formless or Subtle Light (the Golden Flower), the Zen Buddhist satori.

As we move into a world that will become increasingly politically Universalist there will be growing interest in religious Universalism, and in the convergence of different faiths. The Fire is the best basis for such a convergence. 1993 was declared 'a year of inter-religious understanding and co-operation' and the centenary of the 1893 World Parliament of Religions was celebrated in August 1993 in Bangalore, India and Chicago. With a hundred years of the interfaith movement behind us, now is a good time to appreciate that the Fire unites *all* religions and faiths.

The Fire is inspirational in that it enters the soul and inspires, like the Pentecostal Fire. It is the first principle of the Universe

(Heracleitus's Fire), and is behind cosmology, Nature, evolution and consciousness. It is behind physics, biology and psychology, and is the essence of philosophy and restores metaphysics. As the Fire is experienced existentially as a gnosis, it makes possible an existential rather than a rational metaphysics – a supersensible principle that can be experienced. It makes possible a new mysticism and a new universalism and it unites religion and world history. But above all it offers a new way of relating to all humankind, which involves regarding every human being as one's brother at both the political and religious levels.

Sometimes when I look out to sea, the water is a greeny blue and there are no points of light. The sea suggests the physical level of manifest creation, the phenomenal world of Nature. The wavelets push foam gently into the shore, one after another like successive seasons, and there is no hint of the hidden quantum vacuum behind it, the Being behind the Becoming. But it is there. The infinite Fire is always behind cosmology, Nature and history and is the Whole we can glimpse in the mystic vision. It includes the partial perspective of materialism, and unites head and heart.

REDUCTIONIST SCIENCE AND PHILOSOPHY – AND THE FIRE

All enlightened consciousnesses are sure that Nature is a living Being: an organic, living energy which evolves to higher and higher hierarchical wholes. Not all scientists are enlightened, however, and more than 300 years of scientific materialism (from the 1660s to today) have left their legacy. Since 1840 there has been a growing reductionism in science, philosophy and in many other disciplines.

Reductionism describes complex structures in terms of their components, wholes in terms of their parts. From T H Huxley onwards, 19th century biological events were reduced to physical events. In the 20th century, reductionist classical physics reduced the Universe to granular atoms. Reductionist biology and medicine have reduced the human body to a collection of atoms and chemically controlled cells. Reductionist genetics have reduced man to a collection of genes. Reductionist brain physiologists and psychologists have reduced the mind to a collection of neurons and brain-functions. Reductionism assumes that the Universe is granular and materialistic, that it is mechanistic, that the phenomenal world alone is real and that its reality can be apprehended by positivist observation and sense data, the scientist being separate from the granular world he is studying rather than a part of a Whole that includes him.

In philosophy, since 1910 reductionist analytical and linguistic philosophers have analysed concepts and language and have reduced all existing things to observable objects or sense data, and all statements to collections of thoughts or words which they examine for meaning. Any statements which cannot be empirically verified are held to be meaningless. Mystical experience is deemed quasi-empirical or non-empirical and therefore unverifiable, and is excluded from all consideration by reductionist philosophers.

What does reductionism in science and philosophy really mean? For a start, materialists claim to be able to reduce all mental events, including consciousness, to physical events – to the functioning of neurons and electrical discharges in the brain, cells and atoms – with the result that all scientific views of the human being come down to physics in the end. Chemistry, biology, physiology and psychology can all be reduced to physics, and a new unified science of materialistic physicalism is proposed in which neuroscience and neo-Darwinism are very important. The neo-Darwinist Dawkins, the 'neural Darwinist' Edelman, the materialist reductionist Hawking and the reductionist deconstructionist Derrida all seek to explain man in reductionist materialist terms.

The effect has been to devalue man, to dehumanize him. From being the centre of an earth-centred Universe, man has been put on a marginal planet by Copernicus, had his wholeness split into a divided mind and body by Descartes, had his mind reduced to an ape's by Darwin and then split into an unimportant conscious part and more important subconscious and unconscious parts by Freud. Post-Renaissance reductionism has reduced the stature of man, and now man's mind is reduced to neurons and his body to cells and atoms. Reductionism denies that man has a spiritual or divine level, a 'spark in the soul'.

The effect has also been to turn Nature into a dead thing, a mechanism of cells and atoms, the collection of matter that the Romantic poets and Bergsonian Vitalists protested against. The Green Movement knows that exponents of scientific materialism do not understand Nature as comprehensively as the early mystics, such as Hildegard with her *viriditas* or 'greening'.

Where is the evidence for reductionist materialism? It does not exist. To take just two instances, the cornerstone of materialism is that atoms endure, as Whitehead pointed out in *Process and Reality* (2.2.5), but quantum theory and modern particle colliders show that atoms can disappear back into the quantum vacuum from which they manifested as one of a pair of virtual particles. And as for evolution and the idea that we evolved from apes, no one has found a part-human, part-ape skull. To be a reductionist materialist and physicalist seeking a unified theory involves making a leap of belief.

Reductionism is also wrong in its view of the scientist or philosopher as separate from the Universe he is observing by means of physical sense data and measurements. The relativity and quantum theories both regard the observer as being inextricable from what is observed, and particles as being inseparable from the Whole, while Whitehead's philosophy of organism reunites man and Nature in a reality beyond positivism. There is now a belief that the Universe can be understood through reductionist mathematics, but no progress is being made in uniting the four forces of physics. Such a unification is not now expected before 2010, and then we can expect it to be deferred again. Always, reductionism posits a reasoning scientist, whereas the whole man is more than his reason and is intuitively open to forces from the Universe, notably, to the infinite, manifesting Fire.

The Fire which manifests from beyond Nature is the metaphysical first principle: the Fire of Heracleitus, which is also known as the Light. Reductionist philosophers who focused on the rational, social ego and its logical and analytical powers and wrongly debunked metaphysics at the beginning of the 20th century (along with the intuitive part of man which knows the mystic Fire) quite simply threw out the baby of the Fire with the philosophical bathwater, and Western philosophy has never recovered.

As the term 'metaphysics' denotes 'the supersensible' (what lies beyond the five senses) and also a branch of philosophy that includes ontology (the study of Being or Reality) as well as spiritual psychology (universal part of the self that relates to Being at its deepest level), epistemology (what can be known about Being) and cosmology (the structure of the Universe), the Fire is 'metaphysical' in so far as it lies beyond the five senses and is the ontological

Reality which can be known intuitively in the mystic gnosis and which has manifested into the reality behind cosmology, Nature and history. Metaphysics includes every possible concept – not every *existing* concept but every *possible* concept – and a Theory of Everything in terms of the Fire or Light must include many levels: the divine, the spiritual, the psychological, and the physical – the level to which the reductionist materialist seeks to reduce all the higher levels of what is.

The Metaphysical Revolution I launched in 1991 sought to restore the metaphysical reality, the Fire, to its rightful primacy in science and philosophy and to reverse the dehumanizing reduction of man by challenging the post-1840 years of reductionist science and post-1910 years of reductionist philosophy. I have proposed a metaphysical science, an answer to Bergson's call in 1903 for a 'much-desired union of science and metaphysics', and *The Universe and the Light* lists 10 hypotheses (on pp111-2) which are in urgent need of the attention of metaphysical scientists. In many disciplines university syllabuses need to be revised to include the new metaphysical perspective. In philosophy I have introduced Universalism, which asserts that the universal energy of the Fire or Light manifests into the Universe and guides man's universal being. This philosophy addresses the universal being or soul of every human being, regardless of race or religion. This personal approach to the Fire (which Eliot referred to in 'Little Gidding' in his line 'the fire and the rose are one') carries forward the Mystic Revival, for which I have called.

The opposite of reductionism, which reduces a whole to its parts, is traditionally holism, which ascends from the parts to their whole. Often holism and reductionism are two sides of the same physicalist coin. It is possible to be a materialist holist rather than a materialist reductionist, and holists are divided into materialistic holists, who see the Whole as spatial and non-transcendental, and metaphysical holists, whose Whole operates outside (but through) physical laws because it manifests from a metaphysical Reality outside Nature (the Fire). I encompass this second metaphysical holism within my philosophy of Universalism and argue that Universalism is the true opposite of reductionism.

But in the final analysis everything 'reduces' down to a simple polarization: the Fire versus reductionist materialism; or, to put it another way, metaphysics versus materialism.

In fact, materialism is just one level within the multi-level perspective of metaphysics: a physical level of something that has emerged from the more invisible levels of nothingness. In other words metaphysics contains the materialistic level, which has manifested from the Fire. Ultimately, all is One, and the perspective of reductionism is a part of the perspective of the Whole and of the metaphysical vision.

THE LIGHT THAT BECAME THE UNIVERSE

Each Christmas brings cards with traditional Nativity scenes and the participants wearing a halo, a round disc behind their heads as if they are seen against a rising or setting sun. This glorifying halo represents the Inner Light which was once the centre of all religions, including Christianity, Islam, Hinduism and Buddhism. If one closes one's eyes and watches, this Light can flow into the soul so it can actually be seen.

The halo is found in the Roman catacombs and in early Christian Syrian churches. It was widespread in the Middle Ages, and began to die out in art around AD 1450. It was revived from time to time, but has ceased to be the meaningful symbol it once was.

In *The Fire and the Stones* I tried to show that this experience of the inner Light inspired our civilization and 24 others, and made them grow. Someone sees this Light, a new religion and civilization form round it and grow so long as the vision is strong – so long as people go on seeing the Light and passing its energy into their religion and into society. Mohammed saw this Light as a vision of Fire which contained the opening words of the *Koran*. I trace civilizations in terms of this inner Light or Fire and see each one passing through 61 stages, after which it is taken over by another civilization. Civilizations can be compared on the seven-foot-long chart which is sold with the book. The living civilizations, like our own, follow the same stages as the dead ones. This means I can predict the coming stages of living civilizations.

Writing in the 1980s, I was able to predict that the Soviet Union would abandon Communism (as it did under Yeltsin). By seeing this Inner Light as central to the Byzantine-Russian civilization I was virtually the only historical writer to anticipate the collapse of Soviet Communism. I also predicted that there would be a United States of Europe from 1997. This came into embryonic being when the Maastricht Treaty was ratified. I have also predicted that the

US, which is in a global stage, will bring in a world government around AD 2002 and will dominate the world in the 21st century. What happened to the USSR serves to confirm this prophecy.

We are like fish in a fish tank in a dentist's surgery, only we move not in water but in Light. The inner Light that is the halo is actually a flowing into us of an outer Light, an energy that is all round us, which permeates Nature.

The Universe can best be understood by looking at the air in a sunshaft. It is filled with motes of dust one does not normally see. The air around where we are now sitting is filled with invisible specks or particles. They come out of the 'quantum vacuum' and some return to it, while some stay out of it. Nothingness is perpetually becoming something and then nothingness again in less time than it takes to blink.

I believe the infinite, moving Fire or Light became our Universe in this way. The Fire or Light was before everything and is within everything, and we can see it when we look for it, as the saints and mystics of the past did. We can imagine them sitting after dark, watching their 'inner televisions'. Electric light took most people out of their inner souls and stopped them from seeing the Light after about 1880. One can literally be blinded by sight – blinded to our inner being and Light by seeing outside too clearly.

Many who work for a living in factories or driving buses know that there has got to be more to life than the grind of work for forty-five years and then a coronary soon after retirement. The experience of the Light brings peace, inner tranquillity, and wisdom, which flow with it into the mind. People who know the Light feel that life has a purpose, and that they have strange new powers in their minds which enable them to see the Universe as a unity.

All those who have 'died' for a few minutes in car accidents or on operating tables and have then come back to life again report going down a tunnel towards a brilliant Light. It seems we know this Light when we die. This Light suggests that we survive death, that we are meant to be here, that our existence is not just an accident.

THE METAPHYSICAL UNIVERSE AND THE METAPHYSICAL REVOLUTION

Radionics practitioners claim that radionics works because all is energy. They measure the energy systems of living forms (humans, animals, plants and the earth) through a combination of ESP and machines, diagnose changes in the body's electromagnetic field and act on them to produce cures. In a Tradition which goes back to radiesthesia (a form of medical dowsing on the radiation given off by the body which was pioneered in France during the 19th century) and to the San Francisco neurologist Dr Albert Abrams (who held that tissue damage or illness would result in changes in the body's energy field and in the early 20th century invented machines that would assist ESP diagnosis of cell changes and act on the body's electromagnetic field to produce cures), they have found that bodily organs have their own frequencies and that radionics can diagnose and treat patients in their absence. The ability of radionics practitioners to heal at a distance through ESP and a mechanical instrument has defied rational explanation in materialist terms; and some have said that radionics depends on the sensibility of the practitioner as much as on his machine.

Central to the Metaphysical Universe is an energy that originates beyond or outside Nature and manifests into the physical Universe. I see the Universe in terms of the metaphysical Fire or Light, the Fire of Heracleitus, which mystics see in their vision of the divine Light. Some radionics practitioners may be content to understand the energy of the electromagnetic fields of bodies in purely physical (or physicalist) terms, seeing them as instances of an energy that is completely explained by quantum theory and the laws of physics. However, I believe that my metaphysical approach, which involves a new view of reality, goes some way to explaining how healing at a distance works, and may prove helpful to many radionics practitioners.

My Metaphysical Universe is a sea of energy to which we ourselves and all living creatures are connected. It is a sea of Light. This Light comes from beyond Nature and the natural, physical world. It is divine and manifests into it – my Form from Movement theory explains with some precision how. In the interests of simplicity the following summary omits all maths and references to scientists' works (both of which can be found in *The Universe and the Light*).

The Fire or Light was the first principle of an infinite movement, a Nothingness that was infinitely self-aware, the most subtle substance. (The idea of a *moving* first principle would have appealed to Heracleitus, who wrote of 'the ever-living Fire'.) A limitation of movement occurred, and this infinite, moving

Fire or Light manifested into Non-Being, which is a regular movement in the form of a spiral. Out of the interplay between the infinite Fire or Light and limited Non-Being, and as a result of the infinite Fire or Light's pressure on Non-Being, two pre-particles arose. They were symmetrically entangled. The movement of infinite Nothingness on Non-Being exerted pressure and annihilated one of these pre-particles and gave energy to the other pre-particle, which was an empty point (Dante's infinitesimal point), a vacuum, a newly defined Non-Being as opposed to a previously undefined Non-Being. This point spread in all directions and expanded, evolving more and more structure, and gradually became Being. In the language of physics, there was activity in the quantum vacuum. From this implicate order more and more explicate implicate (or defined) orders evolved until Existence arose. This comprised pre-particles, pre-matter, pre-organisms, pre-consciousness. The infinite movement or Nothingness continued to give energy to Being, and form arose when virtual particles emerged from the quantum vacuum in pairs. One particle in each pair had the potentiality to become a real particle – explicate Existence. Real particles emerged simultaneously, and the hot beginning or Big Bang took place. By inflation points became galaxies.

The metaphysical view sees the same manifestational process as applying to organisms. Just as a point from a spiral gave rise to galaxies, so a point gave rise to organisms, which ascended into hierarchical wholes from one organism. The expansion happened as the universal energy of the manifesting infinite Fire or Light flowed into the universal being of all organisms, perhaps via carrier photons. An organizing force beyond Nature thus manifested (and continues to manifest) into Nature, creating and developing self-organizing biological mechanisms.

The same manifestational process applies to evolution. Manifestation describes the evolutionary drive of organisms to higher and higher levels of self-organizing and ascending hierarchical wholes. The organism that became an ape is quite distinct from the organism that became a human being. All specimens and creatures, flora and fauna are processes of self-organization to higher wholes. (A similar manifestational process happened with civilizations. A first vision of the Fire or Light passed into a religion and a first civilization, and civilizations similarly ascended through hierarchical wholes.)

The same manifestational process applies to the brain. The brain is transmissive and transmits consciousness from beyond it, probably through photons above the brain (a 'Bose-Einstein condensate'). The transmitted current of the universal energy pours into the brain, perhaps on carrier photons. The energy stimulates and drives the neurons, pushes them into inter-connectedness and binding. The activity of the neurons is thus a consequence of the process of consciousness, not its generator. Evolution and brain function are consequences of transmissions of the Fire or Light.

The Metaphysical Universe is thus a latent, infinite Fire or Light which has manifested into existence, and the air that surrounds us – the quantum vacuum – is filled with the invisible, infinite Fire or Light. This latent, moving, infinite Fire is seething, sizzling into life, constantly expelling virtual particles from the pressure of the infinite on the expanded point, and these particles have the self-awareness of the Fire from which they emerged.

Instant communication is possible in such a Universe which is a self-entangled, interconnected, moving, dynamic field or network of Light. It has been called a 'cosmic consciousness' (by Bucke in his book *Cosmic Consciousness*, first published in 1900) and a cosmic brain or information-processing system (Wheeler) with one giant thought (Sir James Jeans) – this thought being a constant manifesting into form and growth. The majority of physicists do not want to link quantum mechanics and mind, frowning on the convergence of physics and mysticism that has taken place since Capra's *The Tao of Physics*; David Bohm, for one, sought to keep them separate. However Bohm, whose death has been a sad loss, said, 'Light can carry information about the entire Universe,' and he held that information can move at superluminal speeds, speeds faster than the speed of light. When this happens there can be immediate contact at great distance as time slows down and distance is shortened and the two ends of a light ray have no time between them and no distance. This quantum non-locality is to physics what synchronicity is to psychology.

The invisible, latent, infinite Fire or Light may therefore travel (as it manifests) faster than the speed of actual Light, pouring truth and wisdom into consciousness and information into matter at speeds which can be greater than the speed of Light. According to the metaphysical view, this hidden network of the Light is therefore a network of 'airwaves'.

This Light is around us and permeates us all the time. We are like sea-sponges living in a sea of Light. According to the Metaphysical Universe this Light passes into us, instructing our cells to go on performing and bringing understanding, wisdom and love to us. We can be aware of these powers during meditation, when we shut down our rational, social ego and go behind to our soul and spirit, and open to the Light. *The Fire and the Stones* gives hundreds of concrete instances of what happens. The Light that fills the soul is a dazzling inner sun, and this is an actual, not a metaphysical experience.

The soul is like a Cornish harbour that is subject to the inflowings and outgoings of the tides of Light. We are connected to the sea, but are aware of being filled with it at high tide, if we let it in. Those who live all their lives in their rational, social ego may never know it. The sea is at their walls, and they do not know it, and do not open to the power and wisdom it brings, to the higher thought of its Universal Mind, which is Infinite Spirit.

If we open to it, we are joined to it. At the level of soul and spirit, part of ourselves is at one with this sea, just as a harbour filled with the sea is at one with the ocean, and all oceans. Part of ourselves belongs to this sea, and the sea belongs to that part of ourselves.

When we are connected with the self-entangled sea of Light, then we can send information through it to another being that is also connected to it. The sea is greater than us, so we can ask it in all humility 'Please allow this healing to reach so-and-so who is at such-and-such a place' and the healing energy is carried from us to that person who is at a distance, targeting their energy from the sample of their energy which the healer is holding.

The living Metaphysical Universe with its hidden energies in the air helps us to understand healing that radionics practitioners and patients know work. Healing energy can be transmitted at a distance – and so can prayer. A thought about someone can target that particular person on the airwaves and help them, send them extra energy from the infinite Light all round them. There is a long Western Tradition, which I described in *The Fire and the Stones*, that God is this infinite Light, an immanent and transcendent energy which flows into us as well as remaining outside us and beyond us. (There is also a minority Eastern Tradition stemming from Dionysius the Areopagite that God is the unknowable

Darkness behind or within the Light, but rather than quibble in an area beyond our human experience I am happy to follow the Western Tradition as the Light can be known by us.)

According to the metaphysical approach, the fundamental oneness in Nature and consciousness should not be seen at the merely physicalist level. Reductionism and holism are opposite sides of the same physicalist coin. Reductionism sees Nature in terms of its parts – living, granular atoms – and holism sees Nature in terms of self-organizing wholes. But the oneness of the Metaphysical Universe is beyond holism, for the latent, infinite, eternal Fire or Light is central to it, and is beyond physicalism and Nature.

At its physicalist, manifestational level this oneness is actually an electromagnetic spectrum, which includes Nature and our consciousness. Our consciousness is a spectrum that receives light energy at differing frequencies. This light energy includes natural light and infinite spiritual Light, which the non-finite high frequency part of ourselves can receive along with the healing energy and various "paranormal" energies. Our consciousness, then, is a system of light, a spectrum that has a dense, low frequency part and a spiritual, high frequency part. When we shift the level of our consciousness we shift the frequency of our light and open to high frequency currents of energy. As a result we find an increase in our energy. This is what the patient feels in the course of healing at a distance.

Our brain waves vary from 30 cycles per second to 0.5. Beta and alpha rhythms are between 30 to 8 cycles per second, theta and delta from 8 to 0.5. It seems that the gateway to higher frequency is opened when we shut down our own beta and alpha interference (the rational, social ego) and go into meditative higher consciousness at 4 cycles per second. We are then filled with high frequency invisible rays which energize us. In terms of the diagram opposite, the gateway to global consciousness is just off the bottom.

Diagram opposite shows the electromagnetic spectrum with the wavelengths of different kinds of radiation. In addition to well-known abbreviations the following ones are used: μm=micrometre (micron), nm=nanometre (millimicron).

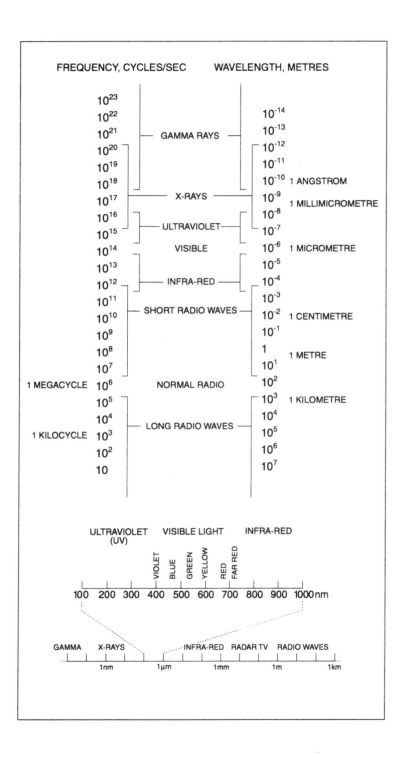

Our brains are surrounded by gamma rays, radio waves and invisible rays of natural light. Among them are waves of manifesting spiritual Light. At the metaphysical level these are unmeasurable; but when they manifest into existence it seems they are off the top of the above diagram.

We receive the full frequency range of the spectrum in the diagram, including the healing and paranormal energies, when we still ourselves to around 4 cycles per second. This gateway opens up our own receiving station to our own consciousness. This is able to receive the manifesting spiritual Light which we receive along with gamma rays, and which we can see with our 'eye of contemplation'.

The shorter the wave length the higher the frequency and the greater is the energy of every photon. When a patient *receives* healing, molecules with low energy absorb photons of high energy which have been channelled by the healer, and they become more energetic and excited. When a healer *gives* healing, the process is of course the other way round: photons of high energy (in the healer) are transformed into lower energy, chemical energy is transformed into radiant energy.

The view of radionics is that each life form has its own electromagnetic energy field within the earth's electromagnetic spectrum, that disease in an organism is caused by a distortion of its electromagnetic field and that each organ has its own frequency. The Metaphysical Universe I have outlined suggests how disease can be detected across the sea of Light by ESP, which is a matching of frequencies, and how electromagnetic fields can be distorted and stabilized.

In absent healing, a wave of light (which is also particles or photons), is sent rippling through the sea of Light to a patient, who receives it at the appropriate frequency. Whether the patient is conscious of this depends on whether he has opened to it around four cycles per second, with his beta and alpha rhythms shut down.

*

It is sometimes said that healing blurs the distinction between mysticism and magic. The difference between the two is that the mystic is subordinate to the sea of Light, and asks 'Please allow healing to happen', whereas the magician subordinates the sea of

24

THE METAPHYSICAL UNIVERSE

Light to his will and says, like Dr Faustus, 'I charge thee' ('I command you'). Most healers are acutely conscious that they are channelling a higher energy for which they have immense respect, and are careful to say 'If it is Your will' and 'Not my will but Thy will be done'.

Healing can seem to blur the distinction because part of the healer's self belongs to the one sea of Light, and it may seem that the healer is asking his higher self, rather than the universal energy, to heal a patient. In fact, the higher self or universal being is a part of the universal energy, and so it is never the higher self alone which is being asked, but the higher or universal being in the context of its relationship with the universal energy of the Light.

The distinction is really between the psychic and the spiritual. The Light of the Metaphysical Universe is a spiritual energy, which can be approached psychically. The psychic frequencies are more dense and longer wave than the high energy spiritual frequencies. The magician manipulates the Light at a low psychic level. The mystic healer requests the Light to act at a high spiritual level. Of the healing energy of the Light, Agnes Sanford writes in *The Healing Light*: 'We have come to the conclusion that a vibration of very, very high intensity and an extremely fine wave-length, with tremendous healing power, caused by spiritual forces operating through the mind of man, is the next thing science expects to discover.' She adds that patients do not feel the high energy but its effect (heat). In the same way we do not see rays of natural light but their composite effect.

The Metaphysical Universe actually operates at four levels. Each level reflects the four hierarchical worlds of the Kabbalah, which are in ascending order: the physical, the psychological (which includes the psychic), the spiritual and the divine. As the four levels include the four hierarchical disciplines which traditionally metaphysics, the branch of philosophy, has followed – cosmology, epistemology (how can I know the Light?), spiritual or transpersonal psychology (locating the soul) and ontology (the Reality of the Fire or Light) – and as metaphysics also means the suprasensible (what is beyond the five senses), the Metaphysical Universe is a Universe whose central Light is hidden beyond the five senses and which includes these four hierarchical disciplines. These relate to the four hierarchical processes of manifestation, which are from end to beginning: Existence, Being, Non-Being and the One.

Metaphysics is a universal science that deals with the laws and structure of *all*. As a rational discipline it therefore includes *all* possible concepts, including infinity. The humanist view excludes the two higher hierarchical levels, soul and spirit, and sees man in terms of body and mind, the physical and the psychological. This view has dominated European civilization since the Renaissance and is responsible for the materialistic, reductionist science which has ruled since c1840 and the materialist reductionist philosophy which has ruled since soon after 1910.

The Metaphysical Revolution seeks to return science and philosophy to the Metaphysical Universe and to effect an abrupt change in the universities. There is no time to wait for a gradual change; the longer we wait, the more people are deprived of the truth about the Universe. The Metaphysical Revolution seeks to relate all disciplines to the One Reality of the infinite Fire or Light, which can be known by the mystics in existential gnosis. (*The Fire and the Stones* contains hundreds of instances.) In the course of establishing the new metaphysical science which Bergson called for in 1903, 'a much-desired union of science and metaphysics', it seeks to review criteria of scientific evidence to include consensual self-reports by mystics who record and report on the Reality of the Fire or Light they have seen.

Verification from sense data is not an adequate criterion for dealing with *all* possible concepts including infinity (the manifesting Fire or Light which can enter the souls of mystics). The Metaphysical Universe demands new criteria of evidence. Materialists will say there is no evidence for the Metaphysical Universe, whereas a metaphysical scientist will say that there is no evidence for materialism, which involves believing, contrary to quantum theory and the practice of particle physics, that atoms endure: Whitehead's 'undifferentiated endurance' (*Process and Reality* 2.2.5) which he held was the 'root doctrine of materialism', the notion that the 'substance' of each atom 'is the ultimate actual entity'. Organizations such as The Royal Society will have to change to accommodate the new thinking. And it is new thinking: the Metaphysical Revolution proposes an entirely new way of thinking about many traditional disciplines.

In *The Universe and the Light* I set out 10 areas which the Metaphysical Revolution urgently needs to investigate in terms of its new assumptions to create a new metaphysical science: the origin of the Universe; the Reality of the microworld of subatomic physics; the electromagnetic spectrum; brain physiology; the relationship between mind and body; synchronicity; mysticism; the Infinity of the Light; evolution; and philosophy as a system of ideas that includes all possible concepts.

My philosophy of Universalism (or Manifestational Universalism) asserts that the universal energy of the Fire or Light manifests into the Universe. The Metaphysical Universe restores a pre-Renaissance view of man in a modern context, and so makes possible a new view of man, who once again has a soul and immortal spirit, and in this respect Universalism carries forward Romanticism, Modernism and Existentialism and goes beyond them in offering a post-Existentialist philosophy. This sees the Universe in terms of the experienceable Light, which is behind history, Nature and cosmology, and makes possible a Mystic Revival.

The Mystic Revival can find its way into any religion. It is a feature of Universalism that the universal energy of the Fire or Light can be received outside all religions. It is the essence of all religions, and can just as easily be received within the context of a religion as outside it.

In the 17th century, the time of the Metaphysical poets, the Light was preached from pulpits throughout Europe. As the vision of the Light fades, civilizations decay, and the Light has been largely missing from Christianity in Europe since 1880. Its imagery has been left behind (for example in the lit candles of the Christingle service).

There are great benefits from being opened to the Light and living in the new centre of the soul and spirit. Everyone is on the Mystic Way, whether they know it or not, and contact with the Light in the illuminative stage which follows purgation and precedes the unitive life removes all psychological stagnancy and brings inner peace, 'the peace that passeth understanding'. Any tendency to depression is removed and in its place comes purposive living. Each influx of the Light brings knowledge and understanding. The sea of energy in which we live is filled with wisdom, and when its tides flow into the rock pools of our souls they leave behind a residue of insight and awareness, like small darting fish and tiny crabs in the crevices of our knowledge. Contact with the Light purifies the senses and the consciousness, and also the higher mind just as an incoming tide cleanses a rocky beach. Hildegard found that she effortlessly understood the psalter and the Bible after her experiences of the Light.

This gift is available to all. The Metaphysical Universe must be proclaimed so that all have the opportunity to open themselves to it. The evidence suggests that only a small minority of people alive today have even heard about it, let alone practise within it. The need for the Metaphysical Revolution is very pressing.

PART TWO

UNIVERSALISM IN PHILOSOPHY

TOWARDS A UNIVERSALIST THEORY
OF EVERYTHING

Einstein arrived at the Theory of Relativity after he lay on his back in a meadow in warm sunshine and wondered what would happen if he travelled back on a sunbeam faster than the speed of light. My Form from Movement Theory can be traced back to two experiences of inner sunshine. As this mystic Light is the metaphysical reality behind the Universe and Nature and its metaphysical perspective makes possible a Theory of Everything, I need to dwell on these two experiences.

I went to work in Japan in the 1960s interested in mysticism, and in Tokyo I met my phonetic namesake, a Japanese expert on Zen called Haga, who invited me to meditate in a Zen meditation centre in Ichikawa city. The seekers were all set a koan (puzzle) and one by one we went up to give our answers. I listened and it was murmur, murmur, murmur, murmur, crack. They were all beaten on their backs. Another man with a stick said to me in Japanese, 'Going up?' I shook my head and got my back as near to the wall as I could. On the way home I discussed the situation with my namesake and he asked, 'Why were they all beaten?' What the beatings had in common was that the beaten spoke so I said, 'Because they spoke. To speak is to incur a beating. The true answer is a silence.' And he said, 'You have understood.'

Next time I went to a Zen temple (Engakuji in Kitakamakura), I shut down my mind and put myself in a waiting silence, and meditating at dawn I saw a glow before my closed eyes. I was writing my poem 'The Silence' at the time, a long poem about the shift I underwent in Tokyo in 1965-6 from the ego to a different centre (the soul or spirit) as I sought the One, and one day after some intense work I was filled with the mystic Light. I quote from my diaries – and the same passage is in *A Mystic Way*, my autobiography:

> 'All morning I have been filled with a round white light:
> I cannot see it, except occasionally when I glimpse it and
> am dazzled, but I know it is there. It is like a white sun.'

After I had come back to England, in September 1971 I had another experience, and I again quote from my diaries and autobiography:

'I now come to the momentous day, Friday 10 September 1971, the equivalent for me of what Monday 23 November 1654 meant to Pascal, who wrote down his experience and sewed the parchment into his doublet and *wore* it until he died, so important was his illumination to him.... I gave my breathing to the twilight until I fell into a trance. And from behind my closed eyes, looking *into* my closed eyes I saw white light, flowing upwards: a tree, white against the black inside me, a bare winter tree of white fire, flowing, rippling as if in water. I put my hands over my eyes, I wanted nothing outside to spoil the brightness of what I saw within, and then, as it were, a spring opened within me... and for a good hour and a half the visions wobbled up inside me like wobbling bubbles... I remembered the first two most clearly: a centre of light shining down from a great height, and then a white flower, like a dahlia or a chrysanthemum, with very detailed, breathtakingly beautiful cells. This was my first glimpse of the celebrated Golden Flower, the centre and source of my being.

'There were too many visions for me to remember one quarter of what I saw. But almost immediately a sun broke through my inner dark and hung in the "sky" with a dazzling whiteness. Then I saw a fountain of light and then all was dark and I saw stars, then strange patterns, old paintings I had never seen before, old gods and saints. When I came out of it, I was refreshed. I felt turned inside out and wobbly at the knees.... I screwed up my eyes to shut out the outer world, and there was a white point, a small circle of light that went deep up into the heavens.... The light moved and changed until it became a celestial curtain blown in the wind, like the aurora borealis.'

That was in 1971, and I have had many more experiences of the Light since progressing along the Illuminative Way to the Unitive Way, on which the Universe is seen as a unity and which changes one's way of looking so that one is the Oneness behind all multiplicity. My autobiography and my Collected Poems capture many of the experiences.

The experience of the Light has long been known and must be fully understood in terms of the Tradition that has grown round it. One literally sees it with one's eye of contemplation, behind closed eyes, when one is at a certain point on the Mystic Way. To see it, one has to shift back from one's rational, social ego into one's soul, one's universal being, and sit and wait for it to come down. In parts of the East the movement is upward, by opening chakras to let Kundalini rise, but there are dangers connected with too early a raising of Kundalini to the crown. The safest way is to sit quietly in meditation or lie on a bed with one's arm over one's eyes and let in the Light. When it comes through, at first it is white. It can look like the painting *Emerging* by Marilyn Sutherland. Or like the dome of Il Gésu, Rome, painted by Baciccia, which shows Christ as Light.

One of the best eye-witness accounts is by St Augustine c400:

> 'I entered within myself. I saw with the eye of my soul, about (or beyond) my mind, the Light Unchangeable. It was not the common light of day.... What I saw was something quite, quite different from any light we know on earth. It shone above my mind.... It was above me (or higher), because it was itself the Light that made me, and I was below (or lower) because I was made by it. All who know the truth know this Light, and all who know this Light know eternity.'

Another eye-witness account is by St Hildegard of Bingen c1140:

> 'When I was forty-two years and seven months old, a fiery light (or burning light) of tremendous brightness coming from heaven poured into my entire mind. Like a flame that does not burn but enkindles, it influenced my entire heart and my entire breast, just like the sun that warms an object with its rays.'

St Hildegard *painted* her experience as a fire round the head, and the Light comes from outside her head into her soul. It has traditionally been held to come from an outside source. Christmas cards often show this, for example some from the Duke of Burgundy's *Book of Hours*.

The Light which is outside the soul but linked to it, is actual, not an image, or symbol or metaphor, and according to the Tradition it is divine. It pours into an open soul rather like a sea pouring into a Cornish harbour. According to the Tradition the vision of the Fire or Light has been widely interpreted as being the vision of God: the vision of Bernini's *St Teresa*. The Eastern Tradition associated with Dionysius the Areopagite sees a Godhead or Darkness – I would say latent or potential Light – behind the Light, but God is transcendent *and* immanent, and a transcendent God (or Godhead) is unknowable whereas an immanent God is knowable as the experience of Light. That is what the Tradition claims. As Blake put it, 'God is Light.' This experience has been known in every culture and civilization, and the list of those who have known the experience of the Light is very long.

The mystic Light has properties within it. Wisdom, understanding and healing and regenerative energies flow into the spirit and soul of those who open to it. The soul is the bridge between our eternal spirit and our perishable psychological mind, and when it is filled with Fire we are aware of new powers of understanding in our mind. The experience of the Fire or Light is immensely health-giving. We are refreshed and open to pure energy. When Jung wrote in his commentary to *The Secret of the Golden Flower* that the experience of the Fire or Light instantly solves psychological problems or 'psychic complexities and thereby frees the inner personality from emotional and intellectual entanglements, creating thus a unity of being', he meant that there is an immediate effect on physical behaviour. Those who open to the Fire or Light abruptly give up smoking or alcohol, in some cases they cease to steal or mug, and they sometimes find they have been healed as its energy pours into their diseased bodies. They feel an overpowering urge to serve all humankind and dedicate their lives to humanitarian endeavours. They found institutions.

To know the Fire or Light is a transformative experience. The Fire or Light is known when a soul is in process of being transformed as it passes through the stages of the Mystic Way: from awakening to purgation, to the Dark Night of the Soul, Illumination and the Dark Night of the Spirit, before attaining the unitive vision.

According to the Tradition of the Fire or Light, truth, wisdom, understanding, love and compassion are poured into humankind from the energy behind the Universe. When this happens the Universe is felt to be living and to have a purpose which can be grasped, to which one can relate one's own purpose.

According to the Tradition (which I have stated in *The Fire and the Stones* and *The Universe and the Light*), the Universe is one energy derived from this Fire or Light, and manifested into form from it. It is a network of divine Light as the medieval artists saw, and I have proposed that the origin and the creation of the Universe came out of a primeval *moving* Fire, the Fire of Heracleitus. My Form from Movement Theory (which focuses attention on the four stages of manifestational process) holds that at the very beginning there was an infinite, self-aware, *moving* Nothingness, a latent Fire. A limitation in its movement formed a spiral, a more limited and undefined Non-Being, and as a result of the pressure of the movement on the spiral two pre-particles arose. One of these was annihilated and the other received energy from the pressure and became an empty point or pre-vacuum, a more defined Non-Being. The point spread and expanded and evolved more structure. It became Being: the quantum vacuum from which virtual particles emerged in pairs. Receiving energy, one particle in each pair became a real particle and endured. The Fire was at first transcendent but through manifestation became immanent. The Tradition asserts, then, that in the beginning was the Fire, which was a Nothingness and latent Non-Being, and out of it manifested Being – the quantum vacuum – and Existence: real particles, matter and organisms. Through inflation from the very small to the very large, it is possible that out of such a beginning came galaxies, evolution – and consciousness, which is transmitted to the neurons of our brains. Thus the Fire is all about us, in the air and in living forms. It pours into our beings and animates us.

Such a view is in keeping with much of the Tradition of the Fire or Light, including the Kabbalah, and I have argued that this process created the electromagnetic spectrum, which is on a manifesting scale from high to low frequency; that at one end, beyond gamma, is the Light which is connected with healing energy; and at the more dense low frequency end are the radio and television and microwave waves.

I see the 'metaphysical' – what seems to be beyond physics – as a Whole that includes the divine and spiritual, the psychic (paranormal) and the physical, which are all aspects of one manifesting process from the invisible to the visible. I see the Light as a non-local hidden reality *behind* Nature, from which Nature has manifested, which carries information instantly. In this I am close to Bohm, who was himself close to Einstein, and especially to Bohm's belief that information can travel at instantaneous speeds around such a network ('Light can carry information about the entire Universe'): that when superluminary particles – photons – move at speeds greater than light, time slows down and distance is shortened and the two ends of a light ray have time between them and no distance and so there is immediate contact – quantum non-locality. If the superluminal information transfer theory in physics links to Jung's synchronicity in psychology then we can understand how metaphysical Light manifesting into physical light travels vast distances instantaneously, pouring truth and wisdom into consciousness and the infinite into matter at speeds greater than the speed of light.

The metaphysical Reality is hidden behind the world of appearances, which conceals it just as the character for 'Light', 'Kuang', was hidden between the two Chinese characters 'Chin Hua', 'Golden Flower', when it was considered heretical to speak of the Light in China in the 9th century AD. The Light is similarly hidden within Nature and has to be looked for in Nature, behind appearances.

The metaphysical perspective draws on the perennial wisdom. The four subdivisions of metaphysics – ontology (the study of Supreme Being or Reality, the transcendent or supersensible), transpersonal or spiritual psychology, epistemology (or human psychology, what can be known about Being) and cosmology (the structure of the Universe) – correspond to the four stages of the manifestational process of the origin and creation of the Universe: Nothingness (real nothing, the transcendent moving Fire), Non-Being (the pre-quantum vacuum), Being (the immanent Light) and Existence (the forms of the phenomenal world). This metaphysical scheme has found its way into the perennial wisdom and corresponds to the Romantic poets' vision of the Universe as Spirit – the Light – which emanates from the One.

The metaphysical Reality that is behind Nature is both transcendent and immanent. It can be *known* as the Romantic poets were aware, and it is the 'knowability' of the immanent manifestation of the One (Being, Light) that makes possible a new metaphysical existential philosophy, Universalism. Rooted in religious Universalism (the view that all humankind's souls can be saved) and historical Universalism (the view that everyone in the world should be represented within the pattern of history), Universalism is a global perspective that focuses on all souls in all disciplines. In philosophy it focuses on the Whole, the One, the invisible realm, not just the visible and material, and philosophers seeking to explain the One are Universalists. My own shade of Universalism, which asserts that the universal energy of the Fire or Light manifests into the Universe and guides man's soul or universal being, focuses on an experience that is central to all religions. It is an existential experience that is independent of all doctrines. One can sit in a multi-faith group and experience the Light, and either keep it outside all faiths or take it into the faith of one's allegiance: Christianity, Buddhism, Hinduism or whatever. To put it even more simply, if one sits and opens to the Light and feels it surge in and energize, one is filled with wisdom and understanding from beyond which develop one's living and take it along the Providential path. The Mystic Way thus becomes Providential.

Existentialism had to be replaced as it focused on the rational, social ego (in Sartre and Camus, for example), and not the soul or spirit; and emphasized Existence, the lowest of the four manifestational levels, rather than Being, in which the multiplicity of Existence has unity. (Existentialists such as Sartre are always talking about Being, but usually they do not mean Being in the metaphysical sense, rather Existence.) My Universalism is a philosophy of personal experience of Being rather than Existence; of the Light and therefore of metaphysical reality. Universalists do not approach reality through the rational speculation of Leibniz and Kant, but through the experiential opening of meditation.

Universalism, the philosophy of Being and the Light, connects with the 5,000-year-old Tradition of the Fire or Light which I have documented in *The Fire and the Stones*, and challenges post-1840 reductionist, materialist science, and post-1910 positivist philosophy as I have outlined in *The Universe and the Light*. It challenges both reductionism and holism, for as most of modern science is materialist in its assumptions both reductionists and holists are looking within Nature (Existence) and not in relation to metaphysical Being. Reductionists focus on parts (atoms, cells, neurons), holists on the Whole but at the level of cosmology or *Existence*, not at higher levels of Being. Just as the opposite of Existence is Being, so the true antithesis of reductionism is not holism but Universalism, which can make possible a metaphysical science (see the 10 hypotheses on pp111-2 of *The Universe and the Light*) that takes us back to the concerns of Bergson, who in 1903 called for 'a much-desired union of science and metaphysics', the process physics of Whitehead's *Process and Reality* (1929), and Einstein's search for a unified theory from c1917.

In philosophy, Universalism seeks to return positivist, deconstructionist philosophy to the concerns of William James, Bergson, T E Hulme (in his Bergsonian phase), Whitehead and Husserl, c1910. The Metaphysical Revolution I launched in 1991 sought to restore metaphysics in all the sciences and philosophy, and to return philosophy to the concerns of c1910. The Universalist Philosophy Group of 12 philosophers which met regularly to challenge the materialist orthodoxy in philosophy, including that of Derrida, was arguably the first group of its kind since the Vienna Circle of Ayer and Wittgenstein in the 1930s. All the philosophers involved met every month to state how their own philosophical work fell under the umbrella of Universalism.

Universalism's metaphysical perspective returns the philosopher from the interior of his room (and quibbling about words) to the Universe that can be seen on a starlit night, where his task is to give a coherent explanation for everything in terms of the One. Once again philosophy involves looking at Nature and the Universe and explaining them, as did Plato and the great philosophers. When possible our philosophy group sat in the open air so that the Universe before our eyes was the subject of our discussions, not problems of logic or language. Universalism is in direct contrast to reductionist materialism in science and logical positivism and linguistic analysis in philosophy. In philosophy, Universalism seeks to reverse the work of the Vienna Circle. In science Universalism seeks to reverse not just the Enlightenment, which was a Darkness, but the finiteness of all the materialist developments after the foundation of the Royal Society in 1660 and of the discoveries of the young Newton. In short, Universalism is reversing 330 years of opposition to metaphysics, and returning to the position in the 1650s when the Metaphysical poets of 1600-60 who saw the visible within the context of the invisible were still in their heyday. But of course Universalism goes forward; it returns to the past to obtain its bearings for a correct future direction. Like the Existentialist philosophers, all of whom were different but subscribed to Existentialism, Universalist philosophers all have their own emphasis but subscribe to Universalism.

The battlelines are therefore drawn up between materialism and metaphysics; which is to say, materialism and Universalism. The reductionists are very strong and include many neural materialists and neo-Darwinists who believe that we are living on a 'dunghill of purposeless interconnected corruption'. The Royal Society and Royal Philosophical Society are on their side. The reductionists assert that a Theory of Everything is possible at the lowest of our four levels, cosmology and Existence, and that quite simply the higher levels do not exist as there is no scientific 'evidence' for them. In fact, a materialist 'Theory of Everything' is as far away as ever.

Ranged against them are those Metaphysicals, like myself, who hold that a full Theory of Everything is only possible when *all* disciplines are seen in relation to the Fire or Light (the One), and *all* levels, including the physical level of the reductionist scientists, are taken into account. Metaphysicals hold that, as Einstein and Bohm claimed, there is a hidden variability – which I would say is the principle of the Fire or Light – that gives the lie to Heisenberg's indeterminacy principle. The randomness with which electrons appear to behave may have as much to do with the presence of the invisible Fire or Light (Being) as with the apparently erratic behaviour of electrons (Existence).

I hold that a full Theory of Everything *is* possible, but only by including the higher levels of the manifestational process and seeing them in terms of the fundamental Oneness of *all* creation. Creation includes wisdom, understanding, love, compassion, healing, poetry, and sense of beauty – all the non-materialistic qualities, in fact – along with the highest expressions of religious knowledge, which are spiritual, and the supersensible contacts between our minds and brains, which are 'psychic'. To include everything in 'reality', literally everything – every possible concept including metaphysical and psychic levels of reality – is not easy. Practising, paid scientists and philosophers are understandably very cautious in extending the area of what is permissible in science and philosophy in case they lose their jobs, but as a philosopher and poet who holds no paid post in science or philosophy I can go further than the paid 'professionals' can. And so I have erected a metaphysical model and appealed for a Revolution to bring about a rapid change in both science and philosophy.

The Metaphysical Revolution can lead to a truly universal Theory of Everything, one that includes *all* levels and *all* possible concepts. A true Theory of Everything sees the Universe as a living, organic entity, not as a coincidence of four forces. Hawking claims to be seeking a Grand Unified Theory which will unite three forces, and a Theory of Everything which will unite four forces (not before 2010 at the earliest). But unifying the weak and the electromagnetic forces with the strong force and gravity tells us nothing about where love, prayer and conversation fit in. A true Theory of Everything is a theory of *absolutely everything*, including the highest and most noble ideas, and cannot be found at the physical level, the lowest of the ascending hierarchical levels. It must include *all* four levels, the highest being the divine. There can be no physicalist Theory of Everything. A Theory of Everything can only be metaphysical and include the All.

Metaphysics offers a coherent explanation for *everything*, and a Theory of Everything must therefore include *all* disciplines and every level, including the highest religious level. My approach to a Theory of Everything began by unifying history and religion, metaphysics and mysticism in *The Fire and the Stones*. Subtitled 'A Grand Unified Theory of World History and Religion', it shows the Fire or Light which the mystics see as the central idea of all religions and of 25 civilizations of history, each of which has passed or will pass through 61 stages. The Fire spreads from place to place within each civilization, and in each civilization the vision of the Fire or Light creates a new religion. When the vision of the Fire or Light is strong the civilization grows and when it weakens it declines. By seeing the Fire or Light as central to civilizations – a quite different view from the views of Gibbon, Spengler and Toynbee – I predicted the end of Communism and the ratification of the Maastricht Treaty in preparation for a coming United States of Europe. The unification of history, religion, metaphysics and mysticism was my Grand Unified Theory. *The Universe and the Light* extends the unification to physics, cosmology, biology, physiology, psychology and philosophy to expand this unitive vision. I am approaching a Theory of Everything in terms of the Fire or Light, one that includes *everything* and that creates a *fifth force*, an expanding force associated with light which counteracts the contracting force of gravity and which is the Light itself. In due course I will produce a clear statement unifying all disciplines within a coherent, self-consistent metaphysical-Universalist system.

The important task is to unify all disciplines in relation to an experienceable metaphysical Reality that unifies the divine, spiritual, psychological and physical levels of Being and to show how they are all interconnected. The unification of metaphysics and mysticism means that to know metaphysical Reality the individual must progress along the Mystic Way and be transformed by the Illuminative Way and Unitive Way while conducting his own researches; he must grasp that the 'separate' consciousness and way of looking with which one starts the Mystic Way is quite different from the 'unitive' consciousness with which one ends it. Universalism is, like Romanticism, a philosophy of living – it could be summed up as One-centredness – that affects all the arts. (The Metaphysical Revolution is percolating into universities at a more theoretical level.) However, there needs to be a practical Mystic Revival so that individuals can progress and make their own contact in their souls with the experienceable metaphysical Light. In order that as many individuals as possible can play a part in this new movement, as many people as possible must have direct experience of the Light.

A NEW MYSTIC AND PHILOSOPHICAL UNIVERSALISM:

A SPIRITUAL VISION FOR ALL HUMANKIND (SPIRITUAL, RELIGIOUS, ANTI-ATHEISTIC AND POLITICAL UNIVERSALISM)

'A new Universalism?' If emphasized and intoned in a certain way (a *new* Universalism), the phrase begs the question: how does it differ from old Universalism? The old spiritual Universalism focuses on the spiritual awareness of all humankind, religious Universalism focuses on the salvation of the souls of all humankind, historical Universalism focuses on the history of all humankind and political Universalism focuses on human rights for all humankind. I have extended the concept into a mystic Universalism that is mystic and experiential rather than rational or humanist, and into a philosophical Universalism that replaces Existentialism.

My new mystic and philosophical Universalism is centred on the metaphysical and spiritual Fire, which is perceived as Light. This moving Fire (Heracleitus's Fire) existed before the hot beginning or Big Bang or 'flaring out', and manifested into creation and evolution (as outlined in my Form from Movement theory). It is a hidden reality behind the phenomenal world and permeates the Universe. This Fire radiates into us and is perceived as the Inner or Inward Light. In my mystic Universalism the universal energy of the Fire or Light pours into the universal being (soul or spirit) of man from the Universe, bringing infused knowledge and wisdom. Philosophical Universalism describes a world-view in which the Universe and every creature in it is nourished by the permeating Light.

The vision of the universal energy of the Light, which is an actual, not a metaphorical experience, and is known within, behind closed eyes, is the essential mystical and spiritual vision. Contradicting the Eastern Tradition originating with Dionysius the Areopagite that holds that the transcendent Godhead is darkness, the Western tradition maintains that the immanent God is Light, and if we concentrate on immanence, which we can know and experience – unlike transcendence, which is by definition unknowable – then the Light is central to mysticism, the essence of mysticism. The Mystic Way takes us from awakening, through purgation (the Dark Night of Sense), to illumination and thence via the Dark Night of the Spirit to the unitive outlook, in which the Universe is seen as an underlying unity, and spiritual gnosis of the Light is pivotal, crucial, fundamental. The Light is the spiritual vision for the next century and brings with it the unitive vision of mystic Universalism, which holds that all men can know the unity of the Universe through the vision of the Light, regardless of their religion.

This experience of the Light is common to all mystics and religions. The Inner Light that Quakers are supposed to know is the inner Light Zen Buddhists seek. In *The Fire and the Stones* I have shown that the Light is found in all cultures and civilizations and in all religions, which are central to civilizations; that there is a common mystical basis to all the great religions, that truth is universal and all-embracing. Many faiths, one Light. Mystics have known the one truth of the Light and have expressed it in the language of their own culture. The mystics who have known it include: Patanjali, Zoroaster, the Buddha, Mahavira, Lao-Tzu,

Jesus, St Paul, St Clement of Alexandria, Plotinus, Mani, Cassian, St Augustine, Pope Gregory the Great, Mohammed, Bayazid, Al-Hallaj, Omar Khayyam, Suhrawardi, Hafiz, Symeon the New Theologian, Hildegard of Bingen, Mechtild of Magdeburg, Moses de Léon, Dante, Angela of Foligno, Meister Eckhart, Tauler, Suso, Ruysbroeck, Kempis, Rolle, Hilton, Julian of Norwich, St Catherine of Siena, St Catherine of Genoa, St Gregory Palamas, Padmasambhava, Sankara, Guru Nanak, Hui-neng, Eisai, Dogen, Michelangelo, St Teresa of Avila, St John of the Cross, Boehme, Shakespeare, Herbert, Vaughan, Crashaw, Traherne, Norris, Law, Cromwell, Marvell, Milton, Bunyan, Fox, Penn, Naylor, Mme Acarie, Baker, Pascal, St Francis of Sales, Mme Guyon, Wesley, Blake, Swedenborg, Shelley, Emerson, Tennyson, Browning, Arnold, Newman, Mme Blavatsky, Trine, Jung, T S Eliot – and a host of others who enshrine the best of Western and Eastern culture. All religions have the mystic Light as their central idea: Christianity, Hinduism, Buddhism, Islam, Taoism and many survivals of ancient religions. Because the Light is central to all religions it is also the central idea of civilizations, which rise when it is strong and decline and decay when it is weak.

This experience of the Light is potentially universal to all humankind regardless of what religion a person has. To know the Light each has to move back behind the rational, social ego to a new centre, the soul or spirit which is linked to the heart. This can be done in meditation – in the Quaker 45 minutes of silence, for example. I have to say that on the strength of discussions I have had, not all Quakers are using the silence to seek the Inward Light. Some say they are praying in words, remaining within the rational, social ego. Moving from the ego to the soul is like crossing over the Thames to the other side and opening to the Light of the beyond. All men or women are potentially able to do this regardless of their religion provided they are sufficiently advanced along the Mystic Way, and when their religion is vital it helps them to do this but when it is in decay it hinders them. (A religion is vital when it focuses on its own central idea of the Light, and it is in decay when it has forgotten it.) Illumination does not happen until people are ready, in the sense that they are sufficiently purified within. If a group is ready but has not yet experienced illumination, there is a completely safe technique for bringing the Light into members' souls. If any are illumined before they are sufficiently purified within, their illumination will be followed by further inner darkness, and the need for further inner cleansing.

At the personal level, my Universalism encourages people to see the divine Light and this involves a Mystic Revival which they are at liberty to take into whatever religion they follow. At the theoretical level, my Universalism promotes a Metaphysical Revolution that challenges materialism and reductionism in science and philosophy, and in all disciplines, for the ontology, psychology, epistemology and cosmology of the Universe have all unfolded from, and must be seen within the context of the divine Fire or Light. All knowledge can be reunified in terms of the Fire or Light, which makes possible a Theory of Everything. At the universal level, Universalism contains the essence of all religions which can be experienced in an Existentialist way, and Universalism is nothing if it is not a practical 'philosophy of living'. It is a post-Existentialist philosophy which every human being can take up within or outside any religion provided he or she returns to his or her soul and contacts the Light which is central to all religions and civilizations. The urgent task is to create a network of practical 'schools' where the Light can be taught.

*

Quaker Universalism is primarily a spiritual and religious Universalism, which may widen into a political Universalism. By Universalism Quaker Universalists mean that they give primacy to the assertion that all humankind has a soul that can be saved, not just Christians; that all men and women have spiritual awareness, whether or not they have a religion; and that Christian teaching, though valuable, is not an exclusive path to spiritual enlightenment. Spiritual Universalism focuses on a vision of all humankind, on the spiritual experience of all humankind, and on the soul of each member of humankind. I would say that spiritual Universalism concerns all humankind's contact with the Light, each person's private contact between his or her own soul and the Light; and the belief that all men and women can make spiritual contact with the Light.

The terminology of the Kabbalah sharpens understanding of 'spirit' and 'soul'. According to the Kabbalah the divine Light is received in the spirit and passed to the soul as illumination, whence it pervades the body as enlightenment. Spirit and soul are very precise terms in the Kabbalah, which distinguishes four worlds which manifest in descending order: the divine, spiritual, psychological and physical worlds. The spirit or Greek *pneuma* (the spiritual soul or Ruah in the Kabbalah) is in the spiritual world and is nearest the divine, and is the 'I' that has lived before, the enduring identity that survives death, receives breath and gnosis of the intellectual (or perceptive) vision and opens to the spiritual energy of the divine Light, the Light of the Holy Spirit in Christian terms. The soul or Greek *psyche* ('Neshamah' in the Kabbalah) is in the psychological world and is the mind's animating soul. The soul is a bridge between the finite mind and the spirit, and on death it retracts into the spirit and according to believers in reincarnation will reincarnate with the spirit. The bodily soul or soul of the Greek *soma* ('Nefesh' in the Kabbalah) is in the physical world and involves lower sensation. When I use the term 'spirit' or 'soul' I am thinking of the top two in Kabbalistic terms, which correspond to the Greek *pneuma* and *psyche*.

From spiritual Universalism – the belief that all men can make spiritual contact with the Light – it is but a short step to religious Universalism, and (to go further down the road of formalism) to a Universalist religion. In all religions there are six kinds of religious outlook and possible positions that any sect or group (such as the Quaker Universalist Group) can take:

1 Adherence to one's local tradition, sect, cult, group or church. This involves no Universalism at all, merely keeping one's self to one's self.
2 Emphasis on the universality of the thought of one's local tradition, whether it is the evangelical tradition of the Church or a particular aspect of Quaker thought, or the thought of any group in any faith, with no concessions to other emphases within one's own religion or to other faiths.
3 Ecumenism of one's own religion, for example Christian ecumenism (the *Concise Oxford Dictionary* defines 'ecumenical' as 'representing the whole Christian world; seeking world-wide Christian unity') or Christian Universalism. This involves seeing one's own local tradition as part of a world-wide movement which may operate some centralized control; for example, in the case

of Christianity seeing one's own group or church as part of one Christian Church or Universalist Christian religion under Jesus Christ.

4 Co-existence between all religions. This involves a high degree of religious tolerance, letting everyone do what they want, while at the same time perhaps tentatively working for convergence. Adrian Cairns expressed this position to me over breakfast at a conference at Winchester in early April 1992: 'Everyone can do what they want. Some may prefer scrambled egg to fried eggs, but we're all having breakfast.'

5 Convergence of faiths while recognizing differences. This involves a pluralist position and active exploration of the common ground between religions and the oneness of the divine mystery of the Fire or Light while preserving local or regional differences and recognizing the value of diversity. This is religious Universalism.

6 Syncretism, which regards divine mystery as one and the response to it as one. This is a move away from the diversity of outlook 5 to unity. Syncretism is defined in the *Concise Oxford Dictionary* as the 'attempt to unify or reconcile differing schools of thought, sects'. Some Christian interfaith groups do not like the word, feeling it has a bad name and compromises their position in relation to their central authority, putting groups who espouse it on the margin of their own faiths. There is, however, a spectrum of syncretism which ranges from intention to achievement: from attempting to reconcile faiths at one end of the spectrum, to actually achieving a reconciliation at the other end of the spectrum, where syncretism involves taking the best elements from each religion and creating a single world religion – like combining all the breakfast choices into one cooked breakfast or like making a soup or goulash consisting of ingredients taken from all the world's religions and cultures. This is Universalist religion. It works best at the experiential and mystical level – I would say at the level of the Fire or Light – and when it allows diversity within the attempted unity. It works least well when doctrines are reconciled, for Universalist doctrinal theology exacerbates doctrinal differences.

The Tradition since 1790 shows two main kinds of religious Universalism or attempts to move towards a Universalist religion: radical Christian Universalism (outlook 3) and convergence-syncretism (outlooks 5 and 6).

The history of Christian Universalism goes back a long way. It can be found in the work of Origen of Alexandria in the third century, but as an organized movement within Christianity it began in the US in the 18th century when George de Benneville migrated from Europe to Pennsylvania in 1741 and John Murray followed from England to colonial America in 1770 and preached a modified Calvinism. At the end of the 18th century Hosea Ballou introduced a Unitarian concept of God. In the 1850s when the population of the US was 23 million, the Universalist Church had 700,000 members and was the sixth largest denomination in the country. The Universalist Church of America finally united with the American Unitarian Association in 1961, forming the Unitarian Universalist Association. In the 20th century Christian Universalism is typified by the World Council of Churches, which officially calls itself 'a fellowship of churches which accept Jesus Christ our Lord as God and Saviour'.[1]

Convergence involves looking for common ground between faiths. Syncretism involves attempting to reconcile faiths or achieving the creation of a single world religion by taking the best elements from each religion and fusing them into one. Both these approaches are consistent with the view that there are many ways to reach divine reality, and that all religions are reflections of an original universal religion. Dr Seaver wrote in *World Faiths* (no 99, Summer 1976): 'All formulated religious beliefs, of whatever Tradition, are no more than fragmented facets of... the white light of truth.' (Or Light). The historian Arnold Toynbee began as a Christian and professed Christianity as the only true religion in *A Study of History*, vol 6. But in *A Study of History*, vol 7[2] he proclaimed himself no longer a Christian and held that all higher religions are 'variations on a single theme'. He listed Mahayana Buddhism, Hinduism, Christianity and Islam, and in *An Historian's Approach to Religion* (1956) he added Hinayana Buddhism, Judaism and Zoroastrianism.

After 1945, the UN, which is an embodiment of political Universalism, has embraced the convergent-syncretist approach to world religion which may replace Christianity. H G Wells wrote: 'The coming World-state... will be based upon a common World

Religion, very much simplified and universalized and better understood.' The UN never invokes God and has a humanistic philosophy: the Catholic *The Universe* pointed out in 1953 that 'the United Nations Organization, like the League of Nations, makes no formal acknowledgement of Almighty God and never collectively invokes the Divine Blessing' – the religious symbol in the UN headquarters is the pagan Zeus – and Sir Julian Huxley, a former Director General of UNESCO, wrote that 'the general philosophy of UNESCO should be a scientific world humanism, global in extent' (*UNESCO: Its Purpose and Philosophy*). As it embraces all faiths, the UN can never be a Christian organization. The World or Universal Brotherhood movement was founded at a conference at Unesco House, Paris in 1950 – its supporters included Eisenhower, Dulles, J F Kennedy and Prince Bernhard of the Netherlands – as the spiritual counterpart of the UN World Government or World Federalist Movement.

In the 20th century Universalism has moved away from the Christian tradition to a convergent-syncretistic view of all faiths. A convergent-syncretistic new world interfaith synthesis aims to replace all religions, including Christianity. Collectively known now as the World or Universal Brotherhood, it has grown up piecemeal over the last 150 years. It is as well to remind ourselves of some of these groups. The better known interfaith groups in approximate chronological order have been:

1830   Brahmo Samaj, founded by Ram Mohun Roy.

1844   The Baha'i world faith, started in Persia by 'the Bab', who was executed in 1850.

1875   The Theosophical Society, founded in New York by Mme Blavatsky and Col Olcott.

1892   Oomoto, launched in Japan. It came to prominence in the 1960s and 1970s.

1893   The World Parliament of Religions, held in Chicago, which pioneered religious synthesis. The conference lasted 17 days and was attended at different times by 3,000 people representing Theism, Judaism, Islam, Hinduism, Buddhism, Jainism, Taoism, Confucianism, Shintoism, Zoroastrianism and the three largest branches of Christianity. Ramakrishna's disciple Vivekananda attended. The centenary year of the World Parliament of Religions was organized by an International Interfaith Organizations Co-ordinating Committee, the Chairman of which was Marcus Braybrooke.

1908   The Universal Religious Alliance, started in New York. It promotes annual World Congress of Man assemblies.

1910   Sufism, brought to the West by Hazrat Inayat Khan from India.

Union of East and West, founded by Keir Hardie, Annie Besant, H G Wells and Mrs Gupta in London.

Union of International Associates.

1914   World Alliance for International Friendship through Religion, founded in Switzerland.

Church Peace Union, founded by Andrew Carnegie.

1920   The League of Neighbours.

1922   Neugeist-Bund (a member of the International New Thought Alliance), founded in Germany.

International Fellowship, founded in India.

1923   Universal Brotherhood, founded in Paris.

1924   The World Fellowship of Faiths (or World Union of Faiths), founded in America by an Indian from Bengal (Kedarnath Das Gupta) and the Communist Charles Weller.

1936   The World Congress of Faiths, launched by the British explorer, soldier, diplomat and mystic Sir Francis Younghusband, who lived in Tibet and India and admired the Baha'i faith. The World Congress of Faiths has pioneered the Inter-Faiths Service which merges Christianity into the Universal Brotherhood. Over the years it has been associated with Radhakrishnan (President of UNESCO and of India, and Vice President of the WCF). Teilhard de Chardin was a syncretist and was a founding member of the French branch of the World Congress of Faiths. (The English edition of his *The Phenomenon of Man* has an introduction by the atheist left-winger Sir Julian Huxley of UNESCO.) A recent Chairman of the World Congress of Faiths is Marcus Braybrooke. The World Congress of Faiths has been represented in the USA by the Temple of Understanding.

1937   The Self-Realization Fellowship, founded in the USA by Mukunda Lal Ghosh who took the name of Yogananda.

1944-5   The World Spiritual Council, founded in Belgium. The World Spiritual Council seeks to establish a vast synthesis of the religious philosophies and cultures of East and West, and in 1953 adopted a Spiritual Charter for Humanity which 'marked an important step along the road of religious, philosophic and cultural *Universalism*, parallel to the Declaration of Human Rights proclaimed by the UNO in 1948' (*The Voice*, no 7, September/ October/November 1953).

1950   Union for the Study of the Great Religions, founded at Oxford by Radhakrishnan, Spalding and Canon Raven, and associated with Zaehner (holder of the Spalding Chair).

1959-60   The Temple of Understanding, founded in the USA by Mrs J Dickerman Hollister with US government backing and Rockefeller money. The Temple of Understanding has been officially described as a 'spiritual United Nations' in which 'universal understanding must inevitably replace nationalist limitations'. The Temple of Understanding held its first World Spiritual Summit Conference in Calcutta in 1968. The concluding address was made by Thomas Merton who spoke of recovering 'our original unity' as a result of which 'we are already one, but we imagine that we are not'. Merton travelled from Calcutta to Bangkok and within two months he was electrocuted when he touched an electric fan wire. The fifth Spiritual Summit took place in New York in 1975 and those present included Margaret Mead, Seyyed Hossein Nasr and Pir Vilayat Inayat Khan, leader of the Sufi Order, who spoke of 'Teilhard's *Phenomenon of Man* as being the New Testament of the Age'. The Temple repudiates syncretism (in its extreme sense of fusing religions) and respects all differences – within the context of Thomas Merton's perception of humankind's unity.

There is thus a tradition of convergent-syncretistic interfaith activity, a flow spanning 150 years, and interfaith groups I have not mentioned include the Vedanta, the World Brotherhood of Faiths, the World Spiritual Communist Congress, Union for the Study of the Great Religions, Divine Life Society (founded by Swami Sivananda), International New Thought Alliance, Subud, Universal Golden Rule Crusade, Golden Rule Spiritual United Nations Crusade, the Universal Alliance (based in Algeria), Unity, the Unitarians, and a host of similar bodies in many countries. The many New Age groups need to be mentioned. In November 1968 the Spiritual Unity of Nations held a large American-sponsored conference to formulate 'A New Age World Religion' to complement the New World Order of the Aquarian Age.

The World Council of Churches officially ties itself to Jesus Christ, as we have seen, but in practice it is syncretistic and even agnostic-leaning, and has been in sympathy with Communism. Vasser't Hooft suggests that syncretism is a greater threat to Christianity than atheism. Christian Universalism envisages ecumenism, which is limited to Christians, whereas syncretism includes all religions; but the World Council of Churches has redefined 'ecumenism' to mean fellowship not 'within the different Christian bodies, but within the entire human race' (Dr Norman, second Reith Lecture of 1978) and Universal Brotherhood was launched by the Catholic Ecumenical Movement as Christian Unity and then as an interfaith movement.

Although my mystic and philosophical Universalism belongs to the convergent-syncretistic side rather than the Christian side, it can renew Christianity along with other religions through a Mystic Revival, by taking Christianity and each religion back to its original experience; that is to say, the central experience of its religion and civilization in the Fire. (This experience has been forgotten as its original message has become corrupted over the years.) The Mystic Revival operates at all levels: at the level of local sect, the universality of its thought, Christian ecumenism or Universalism, co-existence with other faiths, convergence, and the spectrum of syncretism (attempting or achieving a reconciliation of all faiths in relation to the common Fire or Light). I would claim that my Universalism is more fundamental than that of many of the interfaith groups because it is based on the fundamental experience of the Light, the common essence of the deepest experience of all religions, rather than on doctrines. I see my Universalism as being the basis for a religious syncretistic Universalism or a Universalist religion with the Fire or Light as the common ground between religions.

A new Universalist convergent-syncretistic religion contains the essence of all religions and is a synthesis of all religions. It is possible to distil this essence, to refine the practice of all religions to reveal their common ground in the Light. This involves a movement back from the rational, social ego to the soul and spirit where the Light is contacted: the Christian soul and Inner Light, Orthodox's Transfiguration, the Hindu Atman, Brahman and samadhi, Tantric Hinduism's Kundalini, the Mahayana Buddhist enlightenment, Tibetan Buddhist Clear Light of the Void, Zen Buddhist satori, the Islamic Sufi fana, the Taoist Subtle Light (or Golden Flower) and Polynesian mana. A universal religion must include all the knowledge and practices that help man open to God, syncretists argue, and Christianity alone is not enough; they hold that universal religion, for example, includes reincarnation.

In spite of the many interfaith groups there is no one Universalist religion today. The New Age movement is syncretistic in bringing together bits and pieces of different religions, but contains 'hocus pocus' that is unacceptable to many people: crystals, astrology, the more pagan elements. A world Christianity which finds common ground with all other religions on the common principle of the Fire or Light could develop into such a Universalist religion, and the World Council of Churches is edging towards this position, although it does not emphasize the Fire or Light. Quaker Universalism can potentially become such a religion if it takes other religions on board and finds common ground with them in relation to the Fire or Light. It can develop into a new Universalist religion in the 21st century if a worldwide movement spreads it.

I see the North American civilization as having a role in spreading a Universalist religion in the course of stage 15 of its 61 stages (see *The Fire and the Stones*). The North American civilization is young, only a quarter through, and it has a global stage ahead of it. If the US dominates the 21st century and brings regions together under one global, albeit indirect, control, then it will need a Universalist religion to find common ground between all the nations and religions of humankind: a kind of religious United

Nations, or rather a United Nations of religion; a One World Church in one of its currently emerging forms. Or a One World Fire or Light which includes each local Fire or Light.

Such a Universalist religion would unify and reconcile all the local, regional instances of the Fire or Light and would operate in relation to local sects as a kind of two-tier system, as happened under the Roman Empire. Then the international Universalist religion of Jupiter touched the local cults. Local individuals continued to worship in their local temple of Isis or Serapis or Zeus, but on certain international occasions there was an identification with the prevailing Jupiter.

The 'One World Fire or Light' of a Universalist religion can be seen beneath each local, regional Fire or Light. Individuals descend within their own tradition or sect, and if they go deep enough they contact a Fire or Light which is common to all traditions or sects. Or as Paul Tillich put it, each tradition can break through its own particularity – into universality. The way to achieve this, he says, 'is not to relinquish one's religious tradition for the sake of a universal concept which would be nothing but a concept. The way is to penetrate into the depths of one's own religion, in devotion, thought and action. In the depths of every living religion there is a point at which religion itself loses its importance, and that to which it points breaks through its particularity, elevating it to spiritual freedom and to a vision of the spiritual presence in other expressions of the ultimate meaning of man's existence.'[3] Such an active breaking through from one's own particularity into a communal and universal Fire or Light begins as outlook 5 of our six religious outlooks (acceptance of diversity), and ends – experientially rather than doctrinally – as outlook 6: locating a spiritual presence beyond all religions, which in itself is one doctrine-free kind of Universalist religion. On this model, all Fire or Light converges deep down but emerges in each one of us, potentially in all human beings, regardless of which local tradition we have.

*

A Universalist religion may be spread by a New World Order's political Universalism. This is a very important aspect of our theme, for it can turn a Universalist religion from an idea into a reality.

America looks set to create a New World Order that will embody political Universalism, which involves a political vision of every human being in humankind. Just as religious Universalism involves seeing every human being in humankind as having a soul and an eternal spiritual worth, so political Universalism involves treating every human being in humankind as having an equal right to justice and human rights: the vision of the UN's Universal Declaration of Human Rights (1948). Whereas in the present world order of one superpower, regional blocs and nation states, such rights are theoretical and not practical for much of humankind (for example, there are not many human rights for some Iraqis), under a New World Order approaching a world government it is conceivable that every human being in humankind will be a citizen of a world state with human rights.

The New World Order can be one of two kinds. On the one hand, it can be overtly *American-led*, in the sense that it will be organized from the US as part of an expansion of the North American civilization (as I have shown in *The Fire and the Stones*). The US is the world's greatest economic power, and with 5 per cent of the world's population its exports are one tenth of the world's total, including one fifth of the world's output of coal, copper and crude oil, and it is ahead of all other countries in technology, which has allowed the precision bombing of Baghdad and precise missions through space. The American civilization is a young civilization with a global stage ahead; like Rome c180 BC after it had won two Punic Wars, it has won two World Wars. (Anyone who said Rome was finished c180 BC would have been wrong because not long afterwards the entire world wanted Roman citizenship, and anyone like Paul Kennedy who says America is finished now is similarly wrong.) On this model the world government will be American-controlled and run from Washington and New York, and just as the US now dominates the UN Security Council, so the New World Order will be US-dominated.

Alternatively, the New World Order can be overtly *UN-led*. It can take the form of a world government under the UN in which all regions of the world will be represented equally, without any civilization controlling or running it even indirectly, and all regions will surrender their sovereignty to it and take part in a kind of global Cabinet. Such a world government has not happened before, and in *The Fire and the Stones* I see the UN-led model as being less likely than the American-led model. Imagine the United Nations solving the world's problems without a controlling power (currently the United States) behind it. Gorbachev said that 'the New World Order means a new kind of civilization' (a speech to the Chicago Council on Foreign Relations on 8 May 1992) but it is more likely to mark the climax of a stage in the American civilization. If there is a UN-led model, it is likely to be a front for the American-led model.

In our time the American-led model and the UN-led model are interlinked. For the UN-led model has a very powerful and hidden international pressure group behind it which has influence over the American President of the day, whoever he is, and over European leaders. Today many are aware of the 'Conspiracy' (Churchill's word in 1920) associated with the Masonic Illuminati who were founded in 1776, abolished and driven underground. There are many books of revisionist history detailing how the Luciferian ideas of the anti-religious Illuminati entered the French and American revolutions – it was the Illuminatist-Masonic Grand Orient Lodge of Paris (originally funded by Meyer Amschel Rothschild) that achieved the French Revolution of 1789 and murdered Louis XVI and his wife Marie Antoinette – and how the ideas of the Illuminati survived. It is alleged that secret societies connected with them and aiming for world dictatorship funded Karl Marx while he wrote *Das Kapital*, financed the setting up of Communism (which was supposed to impose a Communist-led world government under Lenin but failed), and the rise of Hitler (who was supposed to impose a Nazi-led world government – *neue Ordnung* or new order – but failed), and today control the US Government and the governments of many other nations including that of Britain. I dealt with the background to this international pressure group on pp708-15 of *The Fire and the Stones*. For the full historical background, *see* Appendix 2 ahead.

Many books of revisionist history[4] claim that this group of 'insiders', an oligarchy of super-rich international finance-capitalists who destabilize Western civilization and Christianity and fund revolutions, is currently run by the Rothschild family in conjunction with the Rockefellers (which between them effectively combine Esso and Shell oil) through such Rockefeller-financed international organizations as the Council on Foreign Relations, the Bilderberg Group, and the Trilateral Commission. The common goal of all of these is to form a world government overtly under the United Nations (Bush's 'New World Order') with themselves as the real (but secret) rulers of the world. In 1973 a related organization, the Club of Rome, split the world into ten zones in preparation for the coming world government. These are: North America; Western Europe; Japan; the Rest of the Developed Market Economies (Israel, Australia, Tasmania, New Zealand, Oceania, S Africa); Eastern Europe including the free Soviet Union; Latin America; North Africa and the Middle East; Main Africa; South and South Eastern Asia including India; and Centrally Planned Asia (Mongolia, N Korea, N Vietnam and China). Europe is zone two. What these secret committees decide happens shortly afterwards; for example, who is going to be the next US President or European leader, what currency changes or devaluations will take place. In June 1992, for example, the Bilderberg meeting targeted the former USSR's untapped natural resources, which they'd had their eye on for decades, and oil deposits, gold, diamonds, other minerals, furs and timber have been auctioned off to Western investors funded from Wall Street. Hence the former USSR has been brought into the World Bank and IMF, and hence Gorbachev was expected at the 1992 Bilderberg meeting. (Gorbachev first met David Rockefeller and his assistant Henry Kissinger in February 1989.) There is a growing body of evidence as to the Illuminatist rituals in which leading 'insiders' take part. (In the time of Bush, the rituals were linked with 'the Order', a Yale-based secret society in which Bush himself is alleged to have become an initiate in 1948 by lying naked in a coffin.) The UN is to become the overt world government to which all nations will be subservient by the year 2000. It is to have an army with enforcement powers that can act unilaterally anywhere in the world.

There is a plan that by the year 2000 there will be a covert, American-inspired political Universalism or New World Order, ostensibly under a UN-led world government to which all nations will be subservient. This New World Order plans to keep the peace by having a UN army with enforcement powers than can act unilaterally anywhere in the world. The Romans kept the *pax Augusta* by sending the legions to suppress regional rebels such as Mithradates of Pontus, and the UN army will perform a similar role. The day when American and all nations' soldiers wear UN uniform was brought closer by the Gulf War, which changed our attitudes to the military maintenance of global order as the allied casualty toll was only 378 (against the 58,000 who died in the Vietnam War). This war broke new ground as President Bush, a Trilateralist, first obtained UN permission to fight Iraq, then obtained the concurrence of Congress without a declaration of war; in other words, the Gulf War was conceived and fought within a UN context. Speaking at the Oxford Union in 1992, Reagan called for a permanent UN world army to patrol the globe. He spoke for the Bilderberg Group (which wants this) and the New World Order. At the beginning of 1993 a UN tax of three dollars per barrel on Persian Gulf crude oil came into force, and Iraq's war reparations went to the UN and were used to give food to Kuwait. The US forces in Somalia were under UN command and UN forces there intervened uninvited in the domestic affairs of a sovereign nation and imposed a government on it. At the beginning of 1993 the UN Secretary-General Boutros Boutros-Ghali was negotiating with NATO to take over its forces, which would be under UN command and would then be sent to Bosnia, and in April 1993 NATO reconnaissance planes were flying over Bosnia collecting information.

At Evian in 1992 Bilderberg participants called for 'conditioning the public... to accept the idea of a UN army that could by force impose its will on the internal affairs of any nation'. Kissinger (who speaks for David Rockefeller at the Bilderberg Group) said: 'Today Americans would be outraged if UN forces entered Los Angeles to restore order. Tomorrow they will be grateful'. (Gun control legislation interests the Bilderberg Group as it can disarm the American public before the US is forced to surrender sovereignty to its future UN masters and international bankers. The same is true of Britain, where there has already been some gun control legislation.) The 1992 meeting of the Bilderberg Group heard a report of a speech by the UN Secretary-General, Boutros Boutros-Ghali, which called for a permanent force that could 'intervene at local and community levels'. The Japanese government decided to commit Japan's military to UN peacekeeping missions.

*

It seems, then, that America is creating a political United States of the World, which will follow the Club of Rome scheme and will emerge from current power blocs: the United States of North America, a United States of Europe (which the ratification of the Maastricht Treaty has delivered in embryonic form) including Eastern Europe, Russia/Eurasia, Africa (Organization of African Unity), India, South East Asia (SEATO), Oceania, Latin America (Organization of American States), a United Arab and Islamic States, and a Pacific Community of the Far East. A United States of the World was heralded first by the League of Nations and then by the United Nations.

America has always opposed European colonialism, and was in competition with the British Empire in two World Wars and over Suez. Now it welcomes a United States of Europe as a region on the way to a United States of the World so long as the United States of Europe does its own European dirty work, for example reining in Serbia.

America's nuclear umbrella has always shielded Europe during the NATO time, and now it will be renewed, and Europe's wish to be under this umbrella will be intensified by news that, encouraged by Pakistan's example, Moslems are seeking to possess nuclear weapons. America's nuclear dominance has been assured by the abolition of Russia's land weapons which have more than one warhead, the backbone of the former USSR's defence. American power is the strongest force in the world, coupled with American precision bombing and space technology, and America is poised for a new Empire. This may begin with interventions to help the starving. America's invasion of Somalia was a neo-colonialist venture made acceptable by the plight of Somalis deprived of food by African gangsters, and by and large the Somalis were pleased to see the Americans guarantee their food supplies. Bush said in effect that 'because the US is now the world's only remaining superpower it cannot ignore responsibility for grave humanitarian crises in which American action could well mean the difference between life and death for hundreds of thousands of people' (CFR member Thomas Friedman in the *New York Times* days before the Somali invasion). Such an intervention could set a precedent.

The American-led United States of the World is entirely created by the group of American-influenced international financiers who already control the world's finances. A consortium of bankers including members of the Rockefeller and Rothschild families have already funded Stalin and Hitler and sold arms to both sides in the two World Wars, thus increasing their hold over national governments. There is evidence that this group wants a United States of the World with a Central World Bank, and that it is attempting to secure a United States of Europe with a European Central Bank as a stepping-stone. There is evidence that at a meeting in La Toja in May 1989 the decision was taken to proceed as fast as possible towards a European Central Bank, and to overthrow the British Prime Minister Margaret Thatcher as she stood in their way. Since the implementation of this plan through British politicians and the European Commission, there has been resistance from the Bundesbank, which wants to preserve the primacy of the mark as opposed to the ecu and has quietly tried to undermine the ERM by standing aside as all national currencies except the mark have in turn come under pressure. It seems that the Maastricht Treaty is a stepping-stone to a United States of Europe, which in itself will be a stepping-stone to a United States of the World.

It seems that it is in the interests of some of the oligarchic Western finance-capitalists that Islam should be set up as a target or diversion to conceal another global scenario involving arms finance and leading to the destruction of Christian society. It seems that pro-Israeli forces within the West have tried to lure Iran into Bosnia so that a coming US-Iran war can destroy Iran's attempt to possess nuclear weapons and cut Iran down to size like Iraq, and (as in the case of the 1991 Gulf War and the pre-emptive attacks on Iraq in 1993) preserve US-Israeli power in the Middle East. The purpose of America's military reinforcements of Kuwait and Somalia (which President Bush visited) may have been to surround the Moslems – they had two bases behind Moslem lines – and in particular Iran, whose revolutionary guards and troops were based and fought in Bosnia-Herzegovina, in the territory held by Moslems and Bosnian Croats. (At one time they were said to be in the medieval citadel on the hill above Travnik – which was full of young men in combat fatigues wearing green scarves, carrying the *Koran* into battle and taking their inspiration from Tehran – and to be directing two pushes against Turba and Sarajevo.)

In the United Kingdom, as part of this overall scenario, newspaper proprietors who are Rothschild-Rockefeller financed have been destabilizing the monarchy to bring about a republic which will be a pro-American base within Europe. Britain is ruled by bankers via the Treasury. The government has always had a bank manager (Rothschilds) just as Stalin did. The Rothschilds made their wealth in the 18th century in Frankfurt. In the 1850s the Rothschilds' wealth was greater than that of all the European monarchs put together including the wealth of the richest of the lot, the Russian Tsar, which they coveted and acquired. (The target is now the wealth of the British Royal Family.) In Disraeli's time the Rothschilds came up with £4 million at short notice to allow the British government to buy the major holding in the Suez canal. The Rothschilds funded the Bolshevik Revolution and along with the Rockefellers bankrolled Stalin's five-year-plans. They have also been instrumental in creating Israel, both at the time of the Balfour Declaration and in seeking a sympathetic climate for a state of Israel during the war. It was the Rothschilds who wrote a report on British mines recommending 31 pit closures. 'Yes,' the bank manager says, 'you can have your money for schools and hospitals despite your trading deficit, provided you do as we say.' Heseltine attempted to implement the Rothschild report on the British coal industry, which in effect recommended squeezing a national or nation-state industry in favour of world industry (surface coal from Colombia and Australia).

There is a background of Rothschild involvement with the British government. In the 1980s N M Rothschild was behind the Thatcher privatizations of industry, and in 1985 Lord Victor Rothschild personally wrote the Poll Tax, whose unpopularity doomed Thatcher (see Nigel Lawson's memoirs). The same Lord Rothschild was Head of Prime Minister Edward Heath's Think Tank and led Heath into his disastrous confrontation with the miners, and electoral defeat. He also tipped off Philby and denied being the fifth man. Of course he wasn't, he was co-provider of funds for all Stalin's five-year-plans. If anything Stalin was Rothschild's fifth man.

Something similar has happened in the United States. The American bank manager has always been the Rothschild family, who controlled the Federal Reserve System throughout the 20th century, but now the Rothschilds have been supplemented by the Rockefellers. The Rockefellers began oil production in the 1860s and, financed by the Rothschilds, had a virtual monopoly of American oil by 1882. Nelson Rockefeller was Richard Nixon's Vice-President from 1974-77 and introduced Henry Kissinger, a Council on Foreign Relations employee. David Rockefeller has long been President of the Chase Manhattan Bank and the major power behind Esso. He payrolled Krushchev, and Krushchev was dismissed a few days after a visit David Rockefeller made to the USSR in October 1964. David

Rockefeller has long been Chairman of the world government-based Council on Foreign Relations. The Council on Foreign Relations was created in 1921 with Rockefeller family funding and emerged as the American branch and successor in influence of the British Royal Institute on International Affairs (RIIA), which was the brainchild of Cecil Rhodes and which sought to reunite the US with the British Empire, to restore British hegemony over the United States. The CFR created the UN. It is playing a pivotal role in the design of the New World Order. The chief policymaking positions in the US administration are occupied by CFR members. The CFR supplied over 100 officials to Nixon's administration, and has been represented in force in Clinton's administration.

President Clinton was a Rothschild-Rockefeller protegé. Cecil Rhodes' will left his fortune to Lord Rothschild on condition that it should be used to fund Rhodes scholarships for promising New World Order advocates, and Rhodes scholars are trained in the philosophy that the American colonies should be formally reunited with the Rothschild-controlled British Empire (i.e. 'the special relationship'). As a Rhodes scholar Clinton was put through Oxford by the Rothschilds, who identified his promise, with the result that David Rockefeller spoke of Clinton (then a member of the Trilateral Commission) as the strongest presidential candidate. Clinton is also linked to the Rockefellers because Winthrop Rockefeller (brother of David) bought the state of Arkansas as his playground and became Governor. Clinton's Cabinet was almost entirely composed of CFR members and Warren Christopher was Vice-President of the CFR in 1988.

The land for the UN was donated by David Rockefeller's father, and in a sense the UN building is his building. America has always controlled the UN and influenced its main decisions, including the decision to have a Gulf War, which was intended to deprive Saddam (a former CIA agent to whom Britain and America had sold arms during the Iran-Iraq war) of nuclear weapons and therefore give control of Middle Eastern oil to America. President Bush, the implementer of the Gulf War, has had financial backing from David Rockefeller and co-founded his own oil company, Zapata Off-Shore Company, Houston. (The Bush family is one of the 'third tier' dynastic families of the New World Order. The first tier is the Rothschilds and the European nobility, the second tier includes the Morgan, Rockefeller and Harriman families who serve the Rothschilds, and the third tier includes the Bush family who worked for the Harrimans. The Bush family banking house, Brown Brothers Harriman, has been a subsidary of the Bank of England in the US since 1800.) Through the UN the USA has pursued American as well as world government (New World Order) interests.

The Bilderberg Group was first conceived by Prince Bernhard of the Netherlands (consort of Queen Juliana, one of the richest women in the world) and was implemented by Lord Rothschild who, along with Prince Bernhard, was a major stakeholder in Royal Dutch Shell. It is named after the hotel in Oosterbeek, Holland, where the Group first met in 1954. The Group meets annually and until 1971 had 15 American and 21 European members – all bankers, industrialists and economists. Now it is reputed to number 100. Proceedings are secret, and reports are sent only to present and past members. After each meeting something happens on the world scene. For example, after a meeting in the early 1970s America devalued the dollar and approached Red China.

The Rothschild family is the leading European force within the Bilderberg Group and shares power with the American-based Rockefeller empire. It is through the Bilderberg Group that the Rockefellers and Rothschilds have collaborated, for example to increase trade with the Iron Curtain countries in October 1969. The Bilderbergers include the world's oil wealth and banking élites, and co-ordinate the European and American power élites and steer the world towards world government. Because of the Rockefellers' and Rothschilds' banking interest they are able to control the media. Maxwell, Tiny Rowland and Rupert Murdoch (who visited and interviewed Gorbachev shortly before the collapse of Communism) have all borrowed hugely from the banks of finance capitalists and have operated within the context of an emerging world government. The world's press only publish what the Bilderbergers want it to. Clinton, John Smith and Gordon Brown all attended the Bilderberg meeting of 6-9 June 1991 in Baden-Baden, Germany, and Clinton's nickname is 'Bilderberg Bill'.

Many recent events can be understood anew in this context. One such event is the oil crisis of 1974, for which the West blamed OPEC and Sheikh Yamani. The price of oil tripled and with it the Rockefeller-Rothschild profits. As a result money flowed into American banks and was recycled to the Third World, to create the Third World debt crisis. Gaddafi, an Arab Nationalist in the

Nasserite mould whose diplomacy contributed to this crisis, originally had support from the Rockefellers and his pan-Arab ideas are feared by Israel who have arranged for him to be cut down to size by the Americans. Arthur Scargill's British miners' strike of 1984 (which received funding from Libya) must be seen within this Rockefellerite context. The deregulation of the American banking system in 1980 is another such event as is the European Monetary System and Central Bank, which Thatcher's Bruges speech opposed, and as a result of which she fell.[5]

The revelation of President Clinton's affair with Monica Lewinsky can be understood within the context of the current Rockefellerite policy to extinguish and resolve conflicts as a preparation for world government. Clinton has implemented this policy in Ireland, and he has tried to implement it in the Middle East, insisting that Israel should surrender land to the Palestinians. The pro-Israeli Rothschild family has been bitterly opposed to this. (The Balfour Declaration agreeing to set up Israel was addressed to Lord Rothschild.) Israel has long wanted the pro-Israeli Al Gore to be president, and an examination of how Monica Lewinsky came to tell her story suggests that pro-Israeli intermediaries were instrumental in making details public and maximizing their impact. The scandal surrounding Clinton can therefore be seen in terms of the power struggle between the pro-Arab Rockefeller family and the pro-Israel Rothschild family, each of which wants their particular emphasis of world government to prevail.

Having put Clinton in power by splitting Bush's vote with Ross Perot (just as they made sure Blair came to power by splitting Major's vote with Sir James Goldsmith), the Rockefellerite internationalists have decided to wash their hands of his scandal-prone administration and put the Republicans back into office to take the world into a world government. The televising of the tapes of Clinton's testimony before a Grand Jury could have been stopped had they wanted it; the fact that they did not is an indication that they are now backing the Republicans.

The Bilderberg Group is not all-powerful. They try to do things – for example, implement a UN army[6] – but they do not always succeed, sometimes because of in-fighting between the Rockefeller and Rothschild contingents. In 1991 they backed Gorbachev and a couple of months later he was overthrown by Yeltsin (whom they subsequently backed). They also wanted Denmark to ratify Maastricht;

and Britain to stay in the ERM. (On Black Wednesday speculative forces opposed to the ERM, notably the pro-Rothschild Soros, plunged the nation-state currencies into confusion.) They have an aim for 2000 – world government under the overt rule of the UN – but it may not happen. The anti-Maastricht lobby will put a spanner in the works if they prevent the creation of a United States of Europe.

On balance it seems as if it will happen. The Bilderberg Group is arranging to strengthen the CIS (Commonwealth of Independent States) so that they can deal with one central authority. Taxpayers of the 'Group of Seven' countries have bought out the CIS debts ($60 billion) in return for dismantling and demolishing the 25,000 ex-Soviet nuclear weapons, thus making the world 'a safer place'. (400 million tons of plutonium are to be salvaged and sold for use in the atomic energy industry.) At the same time Bilderbergers have pressed for the erection of a nuclear (star wars) umbrella over the West against missiles from upstart Third World countries. Russia's 1998 bankruptcy and 50 per cent devaluation have to be understood within this context.

The Bilderberg Group has made progress towards world government on two fronts. Firstly, by establishing a UN tax that will be a levy on oil and will finance new global progress (transmitting billions of dollars to the Third World) and conditioning 'citizens of the world' to pay tribute. The EC voted in May 1992 to impose a $3 per barrel tax on crude oil beginning in 1993, provided the US and Japan followed suit, and Delors told the Bilderberg meeting that the tax revenues would be turned over to the UN to administer a global energy policy. Secondly, by conditioning the public to accept the idea of NATO becoming a UN army that could, by force, impose its will on the internal affairs of any nation, including the US. At a meeting convened by the Stockholm invitation of April 1991, 36 global leaders called for a 'world summit on global governance' similar to the meeting that established the UN and that which took place at Bretton Woods in 1944 to make financial arrangements for the post-war world. UN resolutions now allow the UN for the first time to enforce nuclear, biological and chemical disarmament in a sovereign nation, e.g. Iraq, and the tension between Saddam Hussein and the UN Inspection Teams regularly dominates the news. In the 40th UN General Assembly session in September 1991, various foreign ministers challenged the concept that sovereignty protects nations when they violate basic human rights. The right to intervene in the internal affairs of states to protect human rights was endorsed by the foreign ministers of Germany, Canada, Italy and Austria. We are all world citizens now. Meanwhile as a half-way measure the Bilderbergers have promoted a European army, which has been formed by forces from France and Germany.

The Trilateral Commission is now more powerful. It began in 1971 in response to Nixon's new policy of *détente* with the Soviet Union and closer relations with China under Kissinger. It includes North America, Europe and Japan. Zbigniew Brzezinski took his concept of Trilateralism to David Rockefeller, who personally organized it: he put it to the Bilderberg conference of 1972 and when it was received enthusiastically, assembled the Commission. It had its first conference in 1974 and is now more interested in North-South economic relations whereas the Bilderberg Group is primarily concerned with East-West relations. Environmentalism is a money-making proposition for interested banks as the Trilateral Commission discovered in April 1990. The UN says the developed nations must spend $125 billion a year to help poor countries clean up their air and water and preserve their forests. Debt forgiveness will be used as a lever to get the poor nations to agree, and the US will finance most of the projects as it creates 20 per cent of the world's pollution while representing 5 per cent of the population (consuming the lion's share of the world's goods and energy as it does). The Commission is now thought of as the Shadow Government of the West.

The IMF and Group of Seven industrialized countries have taken on a world role since the Third World debt crisis and the collapse of the USSR, and have joined the EC's advance to a European Central Bank. All three are now practising a global financial government, and six industrial countries are pulling the strings – as therefore are the Bilderberg Group and Trilateral Commission. The US President's 'advisers' in the Trilateral Commission and Bilderberg Group have urged him to implement the free-trade agreement between the US, Mexico and Canada.

*

There are therefore two New World Orders and two political Universalisms. The first is an overt American-led democratic world government which will bring universal justice and peace in accordance with the United Nation's Universal Declaration of Human Rights (1948) and a common Universalist religion based on the Fire or Light. The second is a UN-led world government which while seeming well-disposed is effectively governed covertly by a moneyed international pressure group which is out to increase its already fantastic wealth.

Any UN-led world government may seem highly desirable, if somewhat impractical and excessively idealistic. Any world government that can solve the problem of the starving in Africa or the refugees who fill our TV screens, seems attractive. The worry is that a UN-led New World Order under the control of an unscrupulous pressure group could lead to a world rule of great dreadfulness, a universal dictatorship worse than Hitler's or Stalin's. Political Universalism of the wrong neo-Fascist kind could lead to the rule of the Beast of Revelations: three and a half years of universal problem-solving and then the great tribulation for another three and a half years, with a Communist-style end of religion, a common universalist anti-religion of power and money with firing-squads at the end of every road. At the Global Deception conference at Wembley, London in January 1993 it was suggested by William Cooper (an ex-US Naval Intelligence officer) that the shadow world government has taken the decision to reduce the population of the world by two billion people – effectively a third of the world's population – by the year 2000, which a Third World War together with AIDS would help achieve. It was suggested that AIDS is a man-made disease created in a Western laboratory before 1970 for world population control, and that it is being used to wipe out large areas of the African and Asian non-productive populations.

The world certainly has a major population problem. The population of the world will have increased from one billion in 1800 to two billion in the 1930s to six billion on 16 June 1999 according to the UN Population Fund, which states in a report: 'Human numbers will certainly reach seven billion. But when the seventh billion is reached and whether world population then goes on to eight, ten or twelve billion depends on policy actions and individual decisions in the next decade.' Some sort of population planning and control is only sensible. But genocide through war, if such a thing is indeed being planned, is not a form of political Universalism right-thinking people will entertain.

The coming New World Order already has an embryonic political Universalist movement other than the UN. It is called the International Society for Universalism, which has its centre in Poland and held its first World Congress in August 1993. It maintains that 'Universalism is the metaphilosophy of the coming European supra-national state' (*International Humanist*, 10, 1990), which is exactly what I predicted in *The Fire and The Stones* (see stage 44 in relation to stage 43). I see Universalism becoming the 'metaphilosophy' of the world.

To which political Universalism does the International Society for Universalism belong? The good Light-based one? Or the other one? Alexander King, co-founder and honorary President of the Bilderberg Group-related Club of Rome which has split the world into 10 zones in preparation for a world government, writes: 'I should welcome with enthusiasm the existence of the International Society for Universalism and its publication *Dialogue and Humanism.*' The provisional theme of the International Society for Universalism's first World Congress in Poland was 'Universal Manifesto – creation of third covenant between man and man'. This coincides with and suggests the humanist approach of the Illuminati. It is important to disentangle illumination from the Illuminati, benevolence from world tyranny. (Compare real enlightenment and the rational Enlightenment which was a darkness.)

In the tangle of proliferating groups we need to be wary. The difference between the two New World Orders and two Universalisms is simple. In the first, man is subordinate to the mystic Light or Inner Light, the central idea of all civilizations (see *The Fire and the Stones*), whereas in the second man is subordinate to witchcraft and the occult rituals of Satan, as are the humanist Illuminati. (See *The Illuminati and Witchcraft* by John Todd, an ex-Grand Druid Council Witch, one of the 13 private priests to the family who rule the Illuminati, under whom come the Council of 33, the 33 highest Masons in the world.) I have reflected the conflict between the two New World Orders in my epic poem, *Overlord*.

Returning to the conflict between Christian Universalism and syncretism, between 'Christ' and 'Belial' (Baal) (*Cor.* 2, 6. 14-17), just as Satan's political fronts are the Trilateral Commission, the CFR, the Bilderberg Group, the Club of Rome and Communism, so Satan is boss of the Brotherhood, whose leaders (referred to as 'the Elder Brethren of the race', 'the Elders', 'the Perfect Ones', 'the Great White Brotherhood', 'The Elder Brothers of Humanity' and 'the Enlightened Ones') are anonymous Illuminati. John Cotter, author of *A Study in Syncretism*[7] puts it more cautiously: 'It may well be that the World Brotherhood and the Illuminati, which many historians have identified as the secret power behind the French Revolution of 1789, are one and the same. It seems the time may be fast approaching when this behind-the-scenes "Brotherhood" may come out into the open as world rulers.'

The Elder Brothers are leaders of the world. Orwell stumbled across this and had O'Brien say in *1984*: 'I can tell you that the Brotherhood exists, but I cannot tell you whether it numbers a hundred members, or ten million.... The Brotherhood cannot be wiped out because it is not an organization in the ordinary sense.' Krushchev was reported as proposing Bulganin for Chairmanship of the Council of Trustees 'on the instructions of the CPU and the Council of Elders', the latter being the leaders of the Universal Brotherhood, a Council that was in a position to give instructions to Krushchev and which is bent on possession of world power.

What is needed is a well-disposed but sensible World Brotherhood purged of dubious political and Masonic parentage, starting afresh with the mystic Light. That is why I propose a 'new' Light-based Universalist religion, whose enlightened leaders can lead the world from the position of a 'good' Universalism. My philosophical Universalism belongs to the good non-Masonic New World Order. As I wrote in my poem 'Archangel':

> 'Into the People's Square,
> From the Cathedral gates,
> File in the morning rush-hour
> An élite of self-made Saints
> Each still on the last hour's quest.
> They reach the central banner
> In the forum of statues and graves,
> The great mazed mandala
> Under which the supplicants wait;
> Decades of contemplation
> Show in their white-haired peace
> As, trusting to perfect feelings,
> They value each equal they greet;
> Until, whispering on silence,

They glide to the Leaders' Hall,
Their hearts, with a World-Lord's wholeness,
At the centre of life, of all,
Their hearts where all past and future meet.'

It is a picture of world government by truly illumined people. I know some denominations such as Quakers are temperamentally opposed to centrally controlled religious conglomerates, but if organizations such as the Quaker Universalist Group go for this option of breaking through their own particularity to the common Fire or Light of a convergent-syncretistic Universalist religion, then they will be confronted by a global scenario. A small group such as the Quaker Universalist Group may have only 300 or 400 members now, but if it stands for this option it can rapidly grow from the small seed it is now to a great tree whose branches can reach round the world.

The 'good' amelioristic European- and American-inspired political Universalism has layers which can be based on the common experience of the Light. It cares about the spiritual Universalism of all humankind – people's openness to the Light – and it can spread a new Universalist religion in which Christianity and other religions meet on the common ground of the Light. Its political Universalism is a genuine American-led (albeit overtly UN-led) democratic New World Order (albeit helped forward by the manoeuvrings of international well-wishers). We must be on our guard against the other genocidal New World Order of the Masonic Illuminati which is a materialistic universalism that is anti-religious and a world totalitarian dictatorship. (For the historical background of this perverse branch of the Illuminati, *see* Appendix 2.) It can be neutralized by a Light-based Universalism. My attitude is that we need to create the good amelioristic New World Order and have a populist watchdog to check that its internationalism is not being abused by a pro-totalitarian genocidal shadow world government.

To translate this into the historical terms of *The Fire and the Stones*, the present stage in the history of the North American civilization, stage 15, will widen into an increasingly global role, while the next stage of the European civilization, stage 43, will see a union, a United States of Europe. In stage 15 there is a new Universalist interpretation of the central idea of the Fire or Light, a development of Christian-religious Universalism that can be expected in the North American civilization; and in stage 44 of the European civilization there is syncretism as religious sects draw together in the shadow of the new conglomerate, and Universalism as the Fire or Light is perceived to be the common source of all religions. This development of a Universalist religion can be expected within the European civilization. (All these developments can be expected to happen anyway, as I have shown in *The Fire and the Stones*.) Against this is an attempt to create a world government that is independent of the civilizations that flow into it, something that has never happened before, and if it is Illuminati-dominated then it will promote the abolition of all the world's religions.

More than ever before, the 21st century will see a struggle between the Way of the Universal Christ and the Way of the Beast. The struggle can be seen as the struggle between the Fire or Light and materialism. It is likely that, on balance, good will prevail over evil. It always has so far. The Illuminatist agent, Lenin, tried to stop religion in Russia ('religion is the opiate of the people'), but after he scorched the earth the grass still grew through again and the churches are now full in Russia. The religious instinct can never be finally suppressed.

The religious instinct, in which the spiritual vision of the Light is central, is fundamental to the philosophy of Universalism and good world government. Conversely, genocidal political universalism is the chief obstacle to the spiritual vision for the 21st century, but I am confident it can be defeated. I offer my new mystic Universalism – the universal energy of the Fire or Light which all countries and cultures have in common – as the force that can permeate the universalism of the atheistic Illuminati and take it over. The philosophy of mystic Universalism is the hope of the future as it offers a new Universalist religion based on the Fire or Light, and a spiritual vision for all humankind. Universalism is an idea whose time has come.

WHAT IS UNIVERSALISM?

Universalism involves a global perspective in many disciplines. Politically it champions universal suffrage: it holds that every human being in the world should have a vote and be regarded as a world citizen, a member of a global community, with human rights to be free from famine, war and genocide; it does not tolerate the alternative concepts of Communism or Fascism, and embodies an ideal the United Nations has failed to live up to. Historically it focuses on the history of the global Whole rather than on the history of separate nation-states, which are an artificial cutting-up of the Whole. Religiously it focuses on the souls of all humankind: everyone's soul can be saved, regardless of whether a person is a Christian, a Moslem, a Hindu or a Buddhist. Universalism is an outlook that sees each human as a global citizen in whatever national history or religion he or she happens to have been born, and not in terms of one particular nation-state's history or religion.

In literature and art it focuses on one ever-present global historical Tradition of metaphysical perception in which Greek and Latin authors are honoured along with medieval, Renaissance and modern metaphysical artists and poets: Homer, Plato, Pheidias, Virgil and Vitruvius along with Dante, Fra Angelico, Michelangelo, Shakespeare, Milton and Eliot. In literature and art Universalists link themselves with the metaphysical perceptions of all cultures. While the ever-present global metaphysical Tradition is the context of Universalist living, each regional locality – which is inextricable from a particular nation-state's sovereignty – has importance for each individual work of art, and local cultural variations are crucial to the panoramic sweep of the Universalist vision. In literature and art the whole global Tradition is a delta of ever-present historical rivers and tributaries, of local regional variations and varieties, and it is the aggregate of these perceived as a Whole that distinguishes the Universalist Tradition.

In philosophy, Universalism's global perspective focuses on the whole Universe. To a Universalist, philosophy returns to the concerns of the great philosophers of the past and describes, and offers a coherent explanation for, the reality of the Universe, not merely patterns of language or logic; and it therefore rejects the outlook of the Vienna Circle. Philosophy is therefore concerned with cosmology, epistemology and ontology. In philosophy the global perspective of Universalism widens into a total perspective, and includes *all* known concepts regardless of whether they can be verified by empirical thought: the seen and the unseen, phenomenal and invisible reality (which can be approached by gnosis), metaphysical as well as materialistic ontology, and a metaphysical approach to the One. Universalism in philosophy has a metaphysical perspective and explores a hidden reality behind the Universe, which it sees as manifesting from the One to the many, from a latent unity to a multiplicity, from the spiritual to the material. It explains what is visible in terms of what is invisible.

Universalism sees this reality as a universal energy that manifests into the Universe and human beings, the One or 'nothing' manifesting into something; a process that explains the origin and creation of the Universe, evolution, consciousness and mind. The universal reality that enters each person's universal being or soul is the Fire or Light that is seen in the mystic vision, and confirms Whitehead's view that 'the purpose of philosophy is to rationalize mysticism'.

Different Universalist philosophers have different emphases. Rationalists, phenomenologists and mystic visionaries approach the One Universe from different angles, and account for its manifesting or emanating – or qualification or differentiation – in their own individual terms. But all have in common a unified view of the Universe in terms of the vision of the One, which is a spiritual reality behind phenomenal existence, and all seek to state a coherent rational basis for it. It is quite new that a number of different philosophers are now coming up with original ontological theories.

Universalism is based on the ontological primacy of an Absolute or One, the ground of Being out of which the Universe and human beings have arisen. The existential foundation of Universalist philosophy focuses on human experience of the One, and its effects. In the past this experience has usually been understood and interpreted in a religious framework. Universalism is independent of established religions, but its focus on the One can be helpful to those who already follow a religion.

In restoring a metaphysical perspective to philosophy Universalism differs fundamentally from current strands in Western philosophy and represents a radical new approach to traditional philosophical problems. It combines the best of Eastern and Western philosophy and acts as a bridge between East and West. Universalist philosophy is profoundly at odds with the assumptions that underlie contemporary science, which are predominantly reductionist and materialist. Many long-standing problems in the prevailing science-based world view (such as the relationship between mind and body, the origin of consciousness and the emergence of values) become soluble from this new perspective. Universalism rejects the verifiability principle of the sceptical Vienna Circle and the falsifiability principle of Popper for a 'gnostifiability' principle: a tradition of existentially practisable 'gnosis' of reality that offers a consensus of reports on inner experience of an Absolute or One, which must be considered by science.

The Universalist metaphysical perspective suggests a single origin in the One and a fundamental connectedness within the Universe. This has ethical implications. Because each human being has a spiritual as well as a psychological-physical identity, origin and connectedness, he or she has a sacrosanct and sacred right to a life free from violence, starvation and genocide. Universalist rulers have an obligation to avoid wars and famines in a benevolent global alliance, and all citizens have a duty to live by peaceful values based on awareness of man's spiritual and metaphysical identity. Because all creatures manifest from the One, they have One-nature, and so Universalists have reverence for life in all creatures.

Universalism's time is coming, for as the world moves towards a single political organization or global polity, the political, historical and religious outlook and philosophy of the new organization will be universalist, and an awakening spiritual-metaphysical awareness of man's universal being will convert an outlook that is latently universalist into an overtly Universalist outlook. Universalism can be the most important philosophy of the 21st century. It is the exact opposite of Communism, which was materialistic and dictatorial. Universalism is metaphysical, not materialistic, and based on universal suffrage, not universal slavery, on a dialectical metaphysics (the One as a synthesis of the spiritual and material) rather than a dialectical materialism. In its purest and most benevolent, internationalist form Universalism can be the coming philosophy of the United Nations.

Universalism embraces all nations, all histories, all religions and all conceptual levels of reality from the One through non-Being to Being and Existence. It explains the Universe in terms of an ultra-material outlook (Being) which includes the material outlook (Existence). Universalism thus perpetrates a Metaphysical Revolution against reductionism, scepticism and materialism and offers a radical alternative to the reductionist and materialist approaches which dominate science, and to their view of the relationship between mind, brain and consciousness. Universalism's values also attempt to offer a guarantee of universal safety and satisfaction for all humankind within a benevolently controlled (and reformed)

United Nations, and a way for each human being to grasp and realize his or her metaphysical identity.

Universalism has replaced Existentialism, holism and many other isms with an experienceable gnosis of reality which is both vertical (the vision of the One and a connected Universe) and horizontal (a notion of world brotherhood).

A PHILOSOPHY OF FIRE

The Fire that has been known since the beginnings of philosophy and has been held to be the first principle – the Fire of Heracleitus – enters our souls when we are ready to open to it. One's first glimpse of it can be the high point of one's life. Pascal's first experience of the Fire was so important to him that he wept: 'The year of grace 1654, Monday, 23 November... From about half past ten in the evening until about half past twelve FIRE. Tears of joy.' His separation from the Fire was at an end: he ceased to be ego-centred and joyfully opened to it and united with it, and was filled with its energy. He wrote the details down and sewed the parchment into the lining of his doublet and wore it for the last eight years of his life.

Hundreds of instances of this actual experience can be found in all cultures and all times during the last 5,000 years. One of the most touching experiences is in the Egyptian *Book of the Dead*: 'I, even I, am the Akh (Shining One) who dwells with the divine Akh.' As can be seen from the two clearest accounts in the Western mystical tradition – those of St Augustine, who saw it as 'the intelligible Light' and St Hildegard who called it 'the living light' (*see* p32) – this Fire, which is also seen as the Light, appears in the soul as a spiritual sun or white light that is dazzlingly bright. According to the Tradition it is widely regarded as being of divine origin and as coming from the beyond and manifesting into Nature. It is interpreted as such in every religion: it is the Quaker Inner Light, the Christian Divine Light (of Christ, the Light of the World), the Orthodox Transfiguration, Islamic Sufi fana, Hindu samadhi, Tantric Hinduism's kundalini, Mahayana Buddhist enlightenment, the Tibetan Buddhist Clear Light of the Void, the Taoist Formless or Subtle Light (the Golden Flower) and the Zen Buddhist satori. The Christian Tradition of St Augustine, St Gregory and St Bernard regarded the vision of the Fire as the vision of God.

The Fire is seen in the soul with the eye of contemplation, which only opens when the eyes of the flesh (the corporeal or physical eyes) and the eye of the reason are closed. The whole thrust of Zen Buddhism, to take one approach, is to shut down the eyes of the flesh and the reason – the senses and the mind (the rational, social ego) – and open the soul in silence to the Fire which is experienced as enlightenment. To achieve an experience of the Fire, a seeker must have set out on the Mystic Way and awakened from the ego and undergone some inner cleansing, purgation or purification, which involves the detachment of the soul from the senses. The experience of the Fire is the mystic illumination, and it eventually leads to the unitive vision, in which the Universe is perceived to be a unity.

According to the Tradition (the visions and interpretations of 5,000 years of unitive mystics) the Universe originated in the Fire. My process metaphysics describes how. I propose that at the very beginning there was an infinite, self-aware, *moving* Nothingness, a latent 'ever-living' Fire. A limitation in its movement formed a spiral, a more limited and undefined Non-Being, and as a result of the pressure of the movement on the spiral two pre-particles arose. One of these was annihilated and the other received energy from the pressure and became an empty point or pre-vacuum, a more defined Non-Being. The point spread and expanded and evolved more structure. It became Being: the quantum vacuum from which virtual particles emerged in pairs. Receiving energy, one particle in each pair became a real particle and endured. The Fire was at first transcendent but through manifestation also became immanent.

The Tradition and my process metaphysics assert, then, that in the beginning was the Fire, which was a Nothingness and latent Non-Being, and out of it manifested Being – the quantum vacuum – and Existence: real particles, matter and organisms. Through inflation from the very small to the very large, it is possible that out of it came galaxies, evolution and consciousness, which is transmitted to the neurons of our brains. According to the Tradition and my process metaphysics, the Fire is all about us, in the air and in living forms. It pours into our beings and animates us. It is the creative principle which controls our genes and organizes forms, which have (to quote Goethe's letter to Herder of 17 May 1787) their own 'inner necessity and truth'. It is the invisible reality which Plato and his Florentine disciple Ficino knew.

To know the Fire is a transformative experience, and the Fire is known when a soul is in process of being transformed in the course of the Mystic Way. The Fire is a mark of transformation, burning away the impurities of the senses and the mind and offering delicious shafts of sun-like light to the soul and spirit, as if a closed, dark and shuttered room suddenly had the windows thrown open to summer sunlight.

*

The term 'Universalism' has been used of history, to refer to the history of all humankind, and of politics, where it suggests human rights for all humankind. If the plan to build a New World Order under UN control at the instigation of the US, the only remaining superpower, is implemented as intended around 2000, then all humankind will be governed by a world government that will by definition be Universalist. Philosophical Universalism derives strength from historical and political Universalism.

The new philosophy of Universalism addresses the Universe and the condition of all humankind in its multi-layered totality, and seeks to give a coherent explanation for its many levels and phenomena, including metaphysical phenomena. In philosophy, Universalism is a movement which offers a *completely universal* explanation for the Universe and humankind's condition, putting the noumenal before the phenomenal. Like the Existentialists Heidegger, Jaspers, Sartre and Camus, or like the psychoanalysts Freud, Jung, Rank and Adler, the new Universalist philosophers each have their own emphasis. But they all subscribe to a unitive view of the Universe. My emphasis is on the universal energy of the Fire. I seek to put the reality of the Fire at the centre of humankind's experience and to see the phenomenal world of the senses in terms of the Fire.

The philosophy of the 20th century has proceeded the other way round, from the phenomenal, not from the noumenal. The logical positivists and linguistic analysts of the Vienna Circle declared invalid any reality that cannot be verified by the senses and confined reality to the phenomenal world, suggesting that any invisible noumenal reality was unverifiable.

In the 1990s the tables were turned. Universalist philosophers have challenged the assumptions that have prevailed since around

1910, when metaphysics was wrongly debunked and philosophy moved away from Bergson, William James, T E Hulme, Whitehead and Husserl. The Universalist Philosophy Group under my leadership included metaphysical philosophers who were neo-Leibnizian and neo-Heideggerian, and philosophers who have produced their own manifestational philosophy. It was arguably the first group since the Vienna Circle (which included Ayer, Wittgenstein and Carnap) to formulate a coherent philosophy that challenges the philosophical Establishment. We took it in turns to give presentations. I spent a whole day giving a presentation and explaining that I put the metaphysical Fire at the centre of the Universe, and that my Universalism asserts that the universal energy of the Fire manifests into the Universe and the universal being (the soul or spirit) with great universality. All humankind regardless of civilization and religion can potentially experience the Fire, which is therefore in-between all religions – independent of them but common to them all. In putting the metaphysical Fire at the centre of the Universe and restoring it to the primacy Heracleitus, Plato and other traditional philosophers once gave it, I seek to reverse the premises of the Vienna Circle.

Universalist philosophers hold that the philosopher can no longer sit in his armchair and quibble about meanings and ignore the larger Universe. American spacecraft are flying between planets and philosophy must include the new cosmological discoveries, the first principles of the Universe, *and* (echoing Whitehead that 'the purpose of philosophy is to rationalize mysticism') the most fundamental mystic experience of the Fire, which is the non-doctrinal common ground of all faiths. Universalist philosophers seek to integrate all these in a universal system. They adopt a cross-disciplinary approach, and have declared a Metaphysical Revolution to bring about an abrupt and sudden change in philosophy as they cannot wait for philosophy to change gradually.

Universalism is a philosophy that is already resonating outside the philosophical cloister, as Existentialism once did.

INTUITIONIST UNIVERSALISM AND THE FIRE BEHIND THE UNIVERSE

I have a photocopy of a chart taken from *The Observer* of 29 June 1958 (the original is yellow with age, having been on my wall at

Oxford later that autumn), 'The "Isms" of Philosophy', which shows the two traditions in modern philosophy that come out of Plato and Aristotle. It shows them in three generations of pairs: Rationalism and Empiricism (17th to 18th centuries), Idealism and Realism (19th and early 20th centuries) and Intuitionism and Logical Analysis (later 19th and 20th centuries). The first in each pair is preoccupied with the ultimate nature of reality and (in varying degrees) with a suprasensible world, a hidden invisible Reality (metaphysics); the second in each pair is concerned with common sense and experience of the natural world, visible Nature alone, what can be verified by the senses. Rationalism shows Descartes, Spinoza and Leibniz; Idealism shows Kant, Hegel and Bradley; while Intuitionism, their most modern descendant, shows Kierkegaard, Nietzsche, Bergson and Sartre.

Universalism is the most recent – indeed, the only recent – flowering of Intuitionism. It is a *metaphysical* development of Intuitionism which is not just about the sensible world. Rationalism, relying on the reason, (I quote from the chart) 'attempted to construct metaphysical systems without relying upon any special form of perception such as intuition or revelation', while Idealism also relying on the reason 'distinguishes sharply between the shifting world of appearance and the world of ideal reality'. Intuitionism expresses (I quote) a loss of 'confidence in the unaided powers of reason' and a drive 'towards the mystical and irrational', 'glimpses of light whose illumination gave one the tone or "feel" of the Universe rather than its structure'. Each has its own special approach and appeal and strikes different chords in people.

Today on the metaphysical (left-hand) side there are essentially two traditions, one older and according to the chart relatively outmoded, the other newer. The first is rational in outlook, based on the rational, social ego (Rationalism and Idealism); the second is based more on intuition and is the culmination of Idealism, Vitalism, the process metaphysics of Whitehead and Existentialism, and looks forward to the next century. The Rationalists approach Reality exclusively through the reason, without relying on any perception such as intellectual intuition or revelation. (I distinguish intellect from reason; intellect is perceptive as in Shelley's 'Hymn to Intellectual Beauty'.) The Intuitionists argue that a person is more than the reason – emotions, feelings, imagination and intuitions as well – and approach Reality through the intellectual intuition, the inner mystical perceptive sense; hence Whitehead's saying, 'The purpose of philosophy is to rationalize mysticism'. The Rationalists build rational systems, like Hegel. The Intuitionists deny systems as do the anti-Rationalist Existentialists.

The revival of metaphysics in the 1990s is something of a coalition. There is a new rational approach to Reality, a rational approach which includes and allows the spiritual, and may be Idealist, but which is still rational. I stand for a more intuitional grounded approach expressed in rational terms, and would go along with Whitehead's dictum, 'The purpose of philosophy is to rationalize mysticism'. To the Intuitionist, the key question is: what is the non-rational, perceptual and intellectual evidence for Being or metaphysical Reality? Universalism seeks to base philosophy on perception or *experience* of metaphysical Reality. Universalism began as a metaphysical movement within Existentialism and it expresses itself in different arts as did Existentialism, so that the Universalist philosopher can express the Universalist experience of metaphysical Reality in literary forms as well as in philosophy: in poems, autobiography, diaries, plays, novels. Universalism is now a new movement in contemporary philosophy in its own right, having replaced Existentialism. Although there is now a coalition between intuitional experience and reason, metaphysical philosophers all share a view of the fundamental oneness of the metaphysical Universe. Whereas non-Universalist philosophers approach metaphysics through 'theories' which are exclusively rational – put forward a premise and see what the result is – Universalism is essentially an existential or experiential metaphysics which, like Romanticism, can be reflected in many disciplines, in the arts, the sciences and meditation; not just within the prison walls of narrow academic philosophy.

Both intuitional and rational approaches are entangled in the various definitions of 'metaphysics'. Early students of Aristotle referred to *ta meta ta phusika*, what comes after physics, the subject dealt with chronologically after the subject of physics. Metaphysics is a branch of philosophy which the OED defines as 'the study of the first principles of things, including such concepts as being, substance, essence, time, space, cause, identity etc.' or 'the ultimate science of Being and Knowing'. From this concern with ontology, the nature of Being, metaphysics came to be regarded as that which is 'beyond' physics, the science of things that transcends what is physical and natural, that which is beyond physicalism, the supersensible – which is how it is thought of in America. The Greek 'meta' means 'beyond' as well as 'after'. It can also mean 'behind', what is behind or hidden within physics; and that is a layer I include in 'metaphysics'. Metaphysics is the study of Being or Reality, or of the first principles of Nature and Thought, which are, I would say, behind or hidden within the Universe. (Interestingly, Einstein said that physics inevitably leads to metaphysics.) As a rational study, metaphysics is the science of the universal Whole or All, and refers to every possible concept: everything that has ever been thought or known about the Universe, *everything*.

All metaphysicians agree that philosophy went wrong c1910. The great philosophers of the past looked at the Universe and tried to give a coherent explanation for it, a coherent description and interpretation. Around 1910, this was still happening. Metaphysics had become exclusively rational and speculative with Leibniz and Kant, becoming a byword for ungrounded speculation without an evidential base, and had fallen into disrepute. Rationalist, ungrounded overturreted metaphysics was bulldozed by the Vienna Circle. Since then branches of Rationalism, sceptical Empiricism, logical positivism, linguistic analysis and deconstruction have concentrated on logical propositions and language, on the words in which reality is expressed rather than on Reality itself and the perceptual experience of Reality. The Metaphysical Revolution has sought to reverse this tendency.

I first used the concept of the Metaphysical Revolution in 1980. It is documented in *A Mystic Way* and in an essay, dated 1980, entitled 'Preface on the Metaphysical Revolution' which can be found on p581 of my Collected Poems. I formally declared the Metaphysical Revolution in April 1991 at the launch of *The Fire and the Stones* in the presence of the historian Asa Briggs and the poet David Gascoyne and others – there is an account of the occasion with pictures in *A Mystic Way*. I chanted Shelley's words in 'The Ode to the West Wind': 'Scatter, as from an unextinguished hearth/Ashes and sparks, my words among mankind', and I have since spoken of the Revolution as scrambling through a hole in the hedge and standing on the positivist lawn.

The Metaphysical Revolution is a reversal of the work of the Vienna Circle, and an attempt to return philosophy to Reality and to the concerns of Bergson, William James, T E Hulme, Whitehead and Husserl, philosophers practising c1910. Metaphysics, as the science of the universal Whole or All, includes every possible concept; not only every concept of what exists, but every concept of what is possible as well. The new philosophical movement of Universalism which is behind the Metaphysical Revolution focuses on the experiential, perceptual evidence for Being or metaphysical Reality, but it is above all an attempt to return philosophy to a study of the *Universe* – the concern of the great philosophers – in all its post-Hubble hugeness. So it includes cosmology and its study of the vastness of space, and all the Universe's visible forms and invisible energies, *everything*. And everything to a Universalist philosopher, all possible concepts, includes spiritual and psychic energies, God, all the 'isms' on the chart, Being, experience of Reality, what is experienced in meditation, Non-Being, life after death, whether or not the actualities have been proved, as well as the physical existence that scientists observe and describe. The metaphysical philosopher, according to Whitehead, endeavours 'to frame a coherent, logical, necessary system of general ideas in terms of which *every* element of our *experience* can be interpreted' (*Process and Reality*, 1929).

The Universalist philosopher who is behind the Metaphysical Revolution sees the multiplicity of the Universe emerging from a unity, sees a One 'Nothingness' manifesting into the many, and attempts to explain the Universe in terms of this process of manifestation. He reveals the truth of the fundamental Oneness of the Universe, which can be experienced, and explains the process of manifestation in terms of a universal energy, a sea of Fire which flows into the universal being or soul of each creature as into a sponge, where it is perceived intuitively, and then reported on rationally. The universal energy flows from the Universe into the universal being, and operates as did Bergson's *élan vital*.

Universalists focus on the perception of the One Being or Reality in the mystical experience. As *The Fire and the Stones* shows, Universalists look at history – every civilization and time – as a whole in their unitive vision, and focus on the experience or perception of the divine Fire or Light. If the many great men (*see* pp41-2) from the Tradition which I state in *The Fire and the Stones* who have experienced and interpreted the Inner Light which is to be found in all the religions were mad, then the best of Eastern and

Western culture is mad. Mystics from all religions have all had the experience of inner illumination after inner purification and have interpreted what they have seen as an experience of Reality or Being, which is described as Fire in the East and Light in the West but which is the same, objective, external, universal energy that flows into the universal being, giving it power of healing and guidance. My own experience of this Fire or Light on Friday 10 September 1971 can be found on pp195-200 of *A Mystic Way* (*see* p31 for an extract). The many 'eye-witness' accounts of experiences of the Fire or Light treat illumination empirically as an actual energy, like the hundreds of instances of the Light seen in the near-death experience, and Universalists hold that such an experience of the Fire or Light is central to all religions and has shaped the rise and fall of civilizations.

Since 1840 reductionist scientists have disqualified reports on the inner mystical experience of Reality as being non-evidential, non-empirical. A feeling is growing among spiritually-minded scientists, however, that this practice is not right and that in a human being who is more than his reason, the rational, social ego is not the sole arbiter of truth and that intuitions experienced in the 'soul' are an equally valid perception of reality, since their quasi-empirical status (the sceptical Vienna Circle's term) can be corroborated by reports from many other mystics which give their experience a full empirical force and status; that both 'outer' and 'inner' ways are differing aspects of the whole person and the whole Universe, and that the philosopher should seek to describe both ways.

This experience of Reality which is central to 25 civilizations is crucial to the new philosophy. It contradicts and belies the assertion of Rationalist, sceptical, Empiricist logic, linguistic analysis and deconstruction that reality is something that can be grasped with words (Derrida's *il n'y a rien hors du texte*). On the contrary, Reality cannot be grasped by the verbal reason, it can only be glimpsed in the silence of the sub-verbal, intuitional, contemplative part of oneself – not by the bodily eye or the eye of the rational mind but by the eye of inner contemplation, which passes it up to reason. Logical positivists, linguistic analysts and reductionist scientists ignore the eye of contemplation. The history of 20th century philosophy after 1910 is based on an ignorance of this inner faculty. Universalists look at man in all cultures and civilizations at all times and connect him to the Universe through the manifesting force of the universal Light which they can experience through the eye of contemplation. By compiling so many reports of experiences of metaphysical Reality and demonstrating their importance to 25 civilizations *The Fire and the Stones* has set the stockade-like outlook of the Vienna Circle on fire and damaged it beyond repair.

The way of intuition in philosophy stands the rational philosophical procedures on their head. Instead of the reason starting with the phenomenal (what is perceptible or evidenced by the senses) and working logically, systematically back to the noumenal (the object of intellectual, in the sense of 'perceptual', intuition which is devoid of all phenomenal attributes), i.e. starting with substance and forms and working back to the first principle; the mystical intuition has glimpsed Reality, the first principle, in what used to be called the Romantic vision, and makes it accessible to the reason, brings the noumenal down to the phenomenal. Phenomenology has a technique which enables us to focus on Reality: Husserl's bracketing. Husserl's phenomenology studies the mind by 'bracketing out' (or forgetting about) the object and focusing on the effect of a perception in the mind. In the same way we can 'bracket out' the source of the universal energy of the Fire or Light – the Absolute – without speculating about its cause, then study its effects in the receiving mind and investigate perceptions and interpretations of the Fire or Light by compiling case-studies.

This method of going straight to the noumenal and bringing it down to the phenomenal can be called 'gnostifiability': using gnosis as an insight which is made available to the reason. It contradicts the Vienna Circle's 'verifiability principle' – that only what can be verified by the senses is real – and conflicts with the procedure of rational phenomenology, whose method is akin to verifiability. Rational phenomenology needs a manifestation and someone to whom it is manifest, as well as structures within the manifest which can be evidentially elucidated, and so a rational phenomenologist has to start with scientific or phenomenal consciousness and trace the process by which transcendental or noumenal consciousness goes beyond the scientific or phenomenal – he has to proceed from the phenomenal to the noumenal. Moreover, a rational phenomenologist holds that to assert with the mystics that the Fire or Light they experience is a universal energy which gives rise to consciousness and matter is, rationally phenomenologically speaking, to speculate in a vacuum. Rational phenomenology requires evidence for Reality, which cannot be 'hypostatized' (i.e. its underlying substance cannot be assumed). But the method of non-phenomenological intuitional or noumenal metaphysics is to proceed from the top down, from a Reality that can be known in the contemplative vision, from the Whole to the parts, from the One to the many, so the Intuitionist retorts with Blake, 'May God us keep/From single vision and Newton's sleep.'

Universalist ontology is how Being or Reality, the Fire, manifests into our Universe and into multiplicity. First there is a Nothingness which is a potentiality, a latent Heracleitan *moving* Fire. Starting with movement stands cause-effect on its head. I know it is possible to see all movement after the Big Bang as a consequence of physical laws set in motion by the Big Bang, and to conclude that there was no movement *before* the Big Bang, but I do not accept that conclusion, and I think of Heracleitus, 'Fragment 30': 'This present world... *has always been*; and is, and will be, ever-living Fire, that blazes with moderation (or measures) and dies down with moderation (or measures).' From this moving Nothingness, this latent Fire, there is then a limitation into Non-Being, which is a potentiality of Being. There is a further limitation into Being, and then into Existence, which begins with the Big Bang. The Fire therefore comes from outside Nature, which it permeates.

It is important to focus in some detail on exactly how manifestation takes place. The key question is how it emerges from before the Big Bang. It starts in transcendence before the Big Bang as a first principle, the latent Fire, a Heracleitan potential Fire, an infinite movement, Nothingness that is infinitely self-aware, a self-entangled energy, the most subtle substance. I know Gödel says that initial premises cannot be explained in full, but I want to get as near to them as I possibly can. All limitations of the first principle are potentialities within it, each of which corresponds to a certain kind of creation, and I propose that within the first principle a limitation of movement occurs in a certain (infinite) region, a modification or qualification that produces a regular movement, and manifests into a multi-dimensional spiral. All irregular movement in this region dies away. This absolute Nothingness always had the potentiality to be limited or modified or qualified, the regular spiral I call Non-Being: a limitation of Nothingness, the Eastern Void which is also a Plenitude, a Fullness.

My view is not dualistic, but it can be said that there is now a kind of duality within the infinite Whole, although one merges into the other, keeping it all One: Nothingness and Non-Being. Both are infinite, but Nothingness is larger than Non-Being and contains the whole of it. Now there is a more definite but still infinite self-entanglement in Nothingness and Non-Being. Out of the interplay between the infinite Fire and limited Non-Being, and as a result of the infinite Fire's pressure on Non-Being, the creative tension between them, two pre-particles arise. These have manifested from the pressure of Nothingness on Non-Being and they are symmetrically entangled. I now propose there is then a reduction of symmetry as a result of the disturbing influence of Nothingness and Non-Being – the movement of Nothingness on Non-Being exerts pressure – and one of the pre-particles is annihilated and gives energy to the other pre-particle, which is an empty point (compare Dante's infinitesimal point), a vacuum, or singularity, a defined Non-Being as opposed to the previously undefined Non-Being.

This point spreads like a multi-dimensional wave in all directions in the field of Non-Being and expands, and gradually becomes Being, the first subtle structure in the vacuum field of Non-Being. Thus from defined Non-Being happens Being. In the language of physics, there is activity in the quantum vacuum. Being now evolves more and more structure as a result of the interplay between itself and Nothingness-Non-Being and the pressure Nothingness-Non-Being exerts on it, and from this implicate order more explicate implicate orders evolve, also due to the pressure from Nothingness-Non-Being, until the explicate order of Existence manifests. (Bohm was very interested in my Form from Movement theory in the last year of his life.)

The process of Being becoming Existence is one in which potentialities become actualities, pre-particles become particles, pre-matter becomes matter, pre-organisms become organisms, pre-consciousness becomes consciousness. The infinite movement of Nothingness and the regular spiral of Non-Being and more defined Non-Being continue to press on Being and give it energy, and form arises when virtual particles emerge from the quantum vacuum in pairs. One particle in each pair has the potentiality to become a real particle, explicate Existence. Such particles emerge simultaneously from the quantum vacuum (Being evolving from within the vacuum field of Non-Being), and as a result of the proliferation of simultaneously emerging real particles (the first multiplicity) there is heat, and the hot beginning or Big Bang or many big bangs as the actual creation of the Universe takes place – out of the *self-aware* infinite Fire of Nothingness: transcendence.

After this event, or these events, there are many more limitations or modifications or qualifications, which throw up space-time, space being the distance between co-existing limitations or events and time being the relationship between successive events in accordance with the anti-Newtonian Leibniz's second letter to Clarke. Each limitation takes us further into multiplicity and a dynamic flux and further away from Nothingness or the One so that Geoffrey Read claims there are now 10^{-23} such limitations per second, 10 thousand million million million modifications per second. In the course of this process, by inflation points in a spiral manifest into galaxies and other points manifest into organisms which have an evolutionary drive and ascend into higher and higher levels of self-organizing and ascending hierarchical wholes, and manifest into our apes and humans, our flora and fauna. I would say that similarly, from other points of consciousness manifests a sea of consciousness equivalent to space, and that the brain is transmissive and transmits consciousness from beyond it. (The movement of civilizations which begin as one glimpse of a point of Light parallels the evolutionary manifestation.)

A complete Theory of Everything starting with the Fire will explain why the Fire manifested into our particular Universe. Clearly, starting with infinite movement and self-awareness and self-entanglement means that there are infinitely possible potential processes, and so why grass, trees, us, our Universe? Why not five-headed human beings who can fly faster than the speed of light? The answer can only come by focusing on manifestations *before* the materialist Big Bang in the pre-Universe before the laws of physics began, where the Universe manifests from a self-aware transcendence into an immanence, from Non-Being into Being, which in turn manifests from the quantum vacuum and beyond Nature into Existence. (The quantum vacuum is in the air in every room now, and while these words are being read virtual particles – I go along with Edgard Gunzig on the existence of virtual particles – come out of the quantum vacuum and return within it, dance like brief motes of dust seen in a sunshaft and die back into it if they do not become real particles.)

A complete Theory of Everything will focus on how the Fire, Universe and consciousness are intermeshed. For the universal energy of the Fire – the first principle that has manifested its substance and its forms of Nature into our Universe, and is at first transcendent and unknowable as a darkness, a Nothingness – manifests into Being and can be known in our existing minds as immanent Light as we have that within us which can know the infinite, as we contain within our finite existences a 'spark of the soul' which can know the moving infinite Being or Light from which we came. (Wordsworth writes of 'A motion and a spirit, that impels/All thinking things, all objects of all thought,/And rolls through all things', 'a motion' which is grasped intuitively and which is not measurable by science, as Wordsworth himself pointed out.) The Universe is metaphysical and purposive and full of guidance and meaning when its ontological origin is seen as I have just described it.

The Universalist ontology is to be contrasted with the positivist view of the Universe, which allows only one stratum, the empirically observable 'outside' forms of the rationally describable Universe, and ignores – indeed, excludes – *all* possible concepts such as Nothingness, transcendence, Being and the like. To positivism what you see it what you get; there is no hidden Reality, and positivists hold that the many poets, artists, mystics and saints who have seen it are all deluded because it can't be objectively verified or subjected to a reductionist scientific test. And so with positivism comes materialism, the theory that the mind, as Crick tells us, is electrical impulses of brain-function, and can be reduced to a part of the body, and neo-Darwinism, the theory that we are mere animals without spiritual perception, like our six million year old ancestor chimpanzee discovered recently in Ethiopia (*Australophithecus ramidus*). Positivism tells us that we cannot evolve organs that can perceive spiritually because there is no spiritual Reality to perceive. In contrast to the Universalist Universe, the Universe is a meaningless 'dunghill of purposeless interconnected corruption' (in P W Atkins' words) if it is seen as an arbitrary consequence of a positivist, materialist, reductionist, physicalist Big Bang.

Intuitionist, mystical, metaphysical Universalism has already stood up to positivism. At the personal level it seeks to bring individuals to an existential confrontation with the Fire or Light through a Mystic Revival. At the social level it seeks a metaphysical revival within all societies and cultures of the world, but particularly in North America and Europe, through the Metaphysical Revolution, a sudden, abrupt change to hurry the process along so that universities include metaphysical as well as secular texts. At the global level, the philosophy of Universalism reflects the metaphysical essence of all religions and involves all the arts and religions in preparing the common ground for the coming world-wide culture. A chart in *The Fire and The Stones* shows the spreading of Fire from culture to culture. Universalism's Mystic Revival, Metaphysical Revolution and cultural synthesis are hastening positivism's demise by restoring metaphysics as the branch of philosophy that studies experience of the first principle of things, the science of Being and Knowing and of the Whole.

At the heart of Universalist metaphysics, then – as in the Middle Ages when metaphysics was the most important discipline in universities – is ontology, its *view* of Being or Reality. In contrast to the positivist ontology, which is entirely physicalist and materialist, the Universalist ontology, as we have seen, envisages the universal energy of the Fire manifesting from transcendence to immanence, where it is perceived as Light, and unfolding all creation, all Nature, consciousness, which uses the brain transmissively, and evolution. To put it another way, the universal energy of the Fire or Light, Being, manifests into the Universe in a process (Becoming), and pours into man's universal being with great universality. The Fire or Light is known epistemologically – seen – by the eye of contemplation, not by the bodily eye or rational eye alone. An epistemology – how we know it – of the Being or Reality behind or hidden within the metaphysical Universe requires intellectual, intuitional knowledge besides rational knowledge, i.e. all the reports of all the mystics. And as a human being is more than his reason – his feelings, emotions, imagination and mystical intuition as well – it is right for philosophy to focus on man in relation to the Universe in terms of *all* his faculties, including mystical intellectual perception, not just the rational, evidential scientific faculty that studies cosmology. The evidence about the Universe must include *all* the reports on *all* the faculties of man. Thus, ontological transpersonal psychology is an important part of metaphysics: the workings of mind-brain in the area where we cross back from the reason to the contemplative, wordless silence of the 'soul' and 'spirit' and approach Reality as gnosis, and then return to report on it and compare reports with other mystics.

Universalist metaphysics therefore approaches the Universe at four levels which are in descending layers: the level of ontology, where it asserts the primary substance as Being or Fire; the level of transpersonal psychology, which investigates where we have the gnosis of Being or Fire in the structure of our psyche – not in the reason but in the 'soul' or 'spirit', the place where in the wordless silence we can perceive the actuality of the mystic Being or Reality, the Light; the level of epistemology, which explores how in the world of Becoming we know Being, gnosis, the mystical vision of the Fire or Light; and the level of cosmology, which takes the world of the physicists, of atoms, matter and substance and asserts that this is ordered and shaped by the latent Heracleitan Fire or Being or Light, and sees the apparent randomness of the uncertainty principle as the effect of pressure exerted by this invisible universal energy.

Atoms were posited 2,500 years ago, but could only be measured in the 20th century; they were a theory for 2,500 years, for which there was no evidence. Nonetheless, they existed. In the same way, I am sure that through advances in technology we will one day be able to record and measure scientifically the workings of this universal energy – perhaps the European Large Hadron Collider will be able to do that and confirm Heracleitus's 2,500 year old view of the Universe as Fire and flux. The universal energy which begins transcendentally and becomes immanent is a very fine and subtle energy, and in the end finds a place beyond gamma on the electro-magnetic spectrum.

The universal energy is universal in the sense that every human being can experience it. Although the soul's contact with the Light is the essence of all religions – the experience of the Light that is fundamental to Christianity (as can be seen in the 14th century mystics), Islam, Zen Buddhism, Hinduism and Taoism – it is generally an experience that happens in one's thirties. Bucke's book *Cosmic Consciousness* records the ages of 43 of those who have had the experience, and they all tend to be in their thirties (some are in their mid-twenties). It is as though one generally has to grow through the selfhood of adolescence before one perceives Reality. The experience is well charted by those who have trodden the Mystic Way. Readers of Evelyn Underhill's *Mysticism* will know that the Mystic Way begins with awakening, that there is then purgation as the sensual ego is cleansed and the 'soul' is detached from its rational dominance in readiness to perceive the Light of Being; that there is a shift from the rational ego to the 'soul', a centre shift, and that there is then illumination with raptures and joys; that there is then a Dark Night, a further purgation or cleansing as the spirit is further removed from the senses and liberated from the rational, social ego. Finally, there is the unitive vision, the butterfly from the sensual, rational caterpillar. I describe the progress along this Way in my long poem, 'The Silence'. All can know the universal energy so long as they grow within.

The unitive vision of the mystics finds expression in Universalism. It is what the Rationalist philosophers have aimed for in their systems, but to a mystic the vision is intuitive, instinctive, natural, there all the time. In the unitive stage, a mystic sees the Universe *instinctively* as a unity, a Whole, from a deeper part of the self than the reason. At the beginning of the Mystic Way, the rational social ego perceives difference, multiplicity, separation; at the end, after illumination, the flowing in of enlightenment, the 'soul' perceives similarities, unity, common ground.

The unitive vision of the mystics coincides with the global vision of Universalism in the same way that St Augustine's *City of God* embodies both a mystical and a global vision. Historical Universalism (which asserts that history must take account of the whole of humankind in relation to the universal energy, not just a tiny part such as the history of Britain) treats history as a whole, as Toynbee sought to do and as *The Fire and the Stones* does. Religious Universalism (which asserts that every human being has a soul or spirit that survives death and deserves to be saved, not just Christian souls or spirits) and political Universalism (which asserts that every human being in the world is a world citizen with certain human rights, including the right to be free from starvation and genocide) both hold that all human beings have come from the One and have a spiritual identity. That means that problems caused by the rise in the world's population in my lifetime from two billion to six billion will have to be solved without manipulating wars, famines, epidemics and plagues to reduce population as if human beings were material or mere animals. Philosophical Universalism sees the Universe including the whole of humankind in terms of the universal energy we can know in the gnosis, and offers a global Existential Metaphysics for the whole person, not just for the reason.

Like Romanticism and Existentialism, Universalism is a philosophy that spreads across the whole of life, way beyond the reason and narrow philosophy. It is therefore cross-disciplinary. It ranges from biology to physics to psychology to religion and mysticism to history; it is pan-disciplinary, for its subject is the entire Universe, and it can therefore be reflected in all the arts. Many poems in my Collected Poems – and I am afraid my poetic output now exceeds Wordsworth's or Tennyson's in bulk – reveal this universal energy, for example 'A Metaphysical in Marvell's Garden' (1980). Autobiography should be about the growth of a whole life at every level and should show the dynamic flow or flux of a life as it happens – which is what I tried to do in *A Mystic Way*. The manifestation and growth process means that the philosopher himself is growing and is a dynamic flow or flux and that his attitudes must be seen within a process, so an attitude he has in 1967 may be different from an attitude he had in 1963, and his growth towards a metaphysical position can be measured – which is what I tried to show in Volume 1 of my diaries, *Awakening to the Light*. All three books are Universalist works. My four volumes of very short stories – 750 stories – reveal Being in glimpses and are Universalist or pre-Universalist works. My poetic epic *Overlord* is also a Universalist work as it describes the Allies' progress in the last year of the Second World War in terms of a metaphysical Universe that includes Heaven and Hell. My two-part verse play about the end of the Second World War, *The Warlords*, a history, looks back to Marlowe's *Tamburlaine the Great* parts 1 and 2 and Shakespeare's *Henry the Fourth* parts 1 and 2. It has over 200 characters and revives verse drama. It is a Universalist work and shows how Universalism can be caught in poetic images.

To the Intuitionist, an image can often reveal Truth more abruptly and stunningly than an abstract statement, which can obfuscate. In *The Warlords* Burgdorf says of Hitler after his death:

'He never grasped that as all are from the One,
Souls are droplets from the divine thundercloud
Which veils the radiant oft-hidden sun,
And returns to it as raindrops evaporate.'

(Part 2, scene 3)

And Montgomery says at the very end:

> 'The only way I can live without a plan
> Is to piece the potsherds of the Universe
> Into the tessellated urn from which they came
> And, like an archaeologist, know its pattern
> In the fresh air of the universal sunshine.'

(Part 2, scene 5)

Both passages are Universalist; the first because it contains an image that reveals Being, the second because it links a sense of purpose to the reality of the Universe.

Universalism is, as it were, a metaphysical holism which sees the Universe in terms of *all* levels. The metaphysical level is missing from holism, which is the opposite of reductionism. Both are two sides of the same essentially materialistic coin, one of which sees matter and organism in terms of parts, the other in terms of the Whole. Universalism is a metaphysical Intuitionism that puts back the levels that are left out of holism.

Universalism has *enormous* potential. It is the only movement in philosophy that is keeping alive the Intuitionist tradition of Bergson, Whitehead and Sartre in contemporary philosophy, but at a metaphysical level. Philosophical movements are always isms: Rationalism, Empiricism, Idealism, Vitalism, Existentialism. Existentialism generally concentrated on Existence and not Being as I have defined it, which represents the higher metaphysical levels. It confused Existence with Being. It focused on the choosing, rational, social ego that interacts with Existence rather than on the deeper 'soul' which can open to Being in meditation. Like Existentialism, Universalism is an umbrella word that can shelter different thinkers under it. Sartre, Camus, Heidegger and Jaspers all had different philosophies, when viewed for differences; but they all have common ground in Existentialism when viewed for similarities. Universalism has already proved resonant, and I have had many letters from people who have read my books and pronounced themselves Universalists.

Universalism's time is coming as we are approaching a period when there will be a move towards a world government – politically North America, the United States of Europe and a coming Pacific Community are to be its backbone in the next few years – and

91

Universalism could become the philosophy of an embryonic world government in the 21st century. Universalists would like to think that Universalism will be as significant to humankind as Communism was in the 20th century. As it emphasizes that all human beings are a multiplicity that has come from a One and have transcendental and spiritual origins, Universalism has a universal application and can work within the philosophical classroom as an Intuitionist statement about all concepts of the Universe – an attempt to reveal the truth about our layered Universe – and at the same time become the philosophy of a more perfect United Nations which respects the sacredness of all human life. Universalism supplies an instant global ethic, for if we are all from the One, we are all brothers and sisters in the One and we all have spiritual identities, and should behave in enlightened ways towards each other, particularly leaders towards the led.

I am not interested in Truth if it makes no difference to me or the world or the common man. Seventy years of analytical linguistic and logical positivism have left our view of the Universe in fragments and relativist confusion. Rational analysis breaks things into pieces, separates phenomena, and is reductionist. Intuition puts the pieces, the separate phenomena, together again in a reverse movement and shows the whole urn from which the potsherds came, and the ghost beyond the urn. It is now time to walk out on the philosopher who sits examining fragments and debating the meaning of meaning in his armchair, and for philosophy to confront and piece together the Universe. The philosopher should sit on the lawn, and give a coherent explanation of the grass, the sky, the blossom round his head, the rose, everything he can see, the Universe in terms of the Whole behind the phenomena, the seemingly unconnected potsherds. To me, one experience, one glimpse, one intuitive insight into, or gnosis of, the Reality or Being behind the Universe that has unfolded into apparently separate but actually interconnected phenomena that are in process is worth weeks of rational systematizing into this category or that, as it shows from perceptual evidence that we are in a metaphysical Universe, subject to the laws of a hidden Reality and part of a process that is purposive, not meaningless. That is why I am in the tradition of Bergson's Vitalism and Whitehead's metaphysical process philosophy rather than in the tradition of Wittgenstein and Ayer, why I am an Intuitionist Universalist philosopher and not a

Rationalist. However, though I ask Rationalists 'On what evidential, perceptual *experience* is your theory based?', like Whitehead I do go along with rationalizing mysticism into a set of general ideas which can interpret every element of our *experience*. I seek to combine the intuitional and the rational in philosophy just as I seek to combine Romanticism and Classicism in my Baroque poetry (see the 'Preface' at the back of my Collected Poems), but my emphasis is on the intuitional side. For me, philosophy is the coherent rational statement of an intuitional, mystical perception of Reality, of the hidden Fire behind or within the Universe.

Universalism is happening and it has been going some years. I have written about it and I shall continue to write about it. There are two hundred books to be published within its sweep. I can do only so much; others should be writing books and coming forward to publish them. We are now as Romanticism was in 1797, and there are literary and artistic developments ahead. How often in a century can one talk of philosophy leading a new movement in the arts? The last time was possibly just after the appearance of T E Hulme's *Speculations*, which together with his imagist poems influenced the Modernists Eliot and Pound. (When I met Ezra Pound in 1970 he told me about the impact Hulme made on him in 1915 – see *A Mystic Way*.) Such a time happens very rarely, once or twice in a century. My message to like-minded philosophers and Universalists is simple. We have a tremendous opportunity to bring about a fundamental change in Western thought, across all disciplines and arts. Something has been started. Each now needs to support what is happening in his or her particular field.

PART THREE

CIVILIZATION AND CULTURE

THE FIRE OR LIGHT AS COMMON GROUND FOR A UNIVERSAL OR WORLD-WIDE CIVILIZATION AND RELIGION

The tradition of metaphysics is dominated by the Fire or Inner Light. From my own experience I became very aware of many paths up one misty mountain – the Sufi and Zen Buddhist paths, the Hindu, Taoist, Christian and Judaistic (Kabbalistic) paths – all of which end in illumination by the spiritual sun. Besides describing how my poems came out of my life, *A Mystic Way* charts my progress to illumination and the process of my unfolding unitive vision, and it describes how after a Christian upbringing I encountered the 17th century Metaphysical poets, whose poems are full of the metaphysical Fire or Light, and how I taught first in Iraq (in Islam) and then in Japan, where I meditated in Zen Buddhist temples and first glimpsed the Light, and how after visiting many cultures and civilizations (including China, the USSR and India) the full experience of the Light took place on 10 September 1971 in a room in London (*see* pp195-200 of *A Mystic Way*). As I reacted to what happened to me I was aware that the experience of the Fire or Light was central to the Christian religion in Byzantine and medieval times (witness the omnipresent halo in art) and was still strong in the 17th century when Fox experienced the Inward Light, but that it has largely been lost from sermons in the 20th century. Whereas it was proclaimed every Sunday in every church in the land in the 17th century, it is missing from the great majority of church services today.

My philosophy of Universalism emerged from 20 years of pondering on this experience of the Fire or Light and the experiences which followed it, some of which can be found in my poems. My philosophical Universalism focuses on the soul of all humanity, on the universal being rather than the social ego, and how it can be filled with the universal energy of the Fire or Light which comes into the Universe with great universality and into human beings of all races, creeds and traditions. I do not say, 'The Inner Light of a particular sect of a particular religion, for example Christianity, alone is true, and we need to consider where that religion stands in relation to other religions and what common ground it has with them, although some do find that the Light *confirms* them in their faith system.' I say, 'The experience of the Inner Light is from the "outer" divine Light which can flow into the soul or universal being of any mystic in humankind, regardless of what religion or credal framework he or she espouses, and mystics of all times and cultures can be invaded by the divine Fire or Light, which is the mover of civilizations.' I hold that 25 civilizations rise from the energy of the Fire or Light, which makes their religions dynamic, and decline when that energy dries up; and that religions, and therefore civilizations, are renewed when mystics contact the Light and put it back into their religion. *The Fire and the Stones* is Universalist in both the historical and philosophical senses – it focuses on the history of all humankind and the centrality of the experience of the Fire or Light – and shows the mystics to be more important to civilizations than generals or economists or politicians.

The new metaphysics has come out of the thinking of a new generation of philosophers. Some are Rationalists who approach Being through the reason alone, and have not necessarily experienced the Fire or Light. I would say that the most interesting are Intuitionists. They have followed on from – indeed replaced – the Existentialist tradition and see Being as the Fire or Light. The Fire is transcendent but as it passes from the One through non-Being to Being and then Existence, it becomes immanent and is experienced within as the Inner or Inward Light. The Intuitionists make the experience of Being – the Fire or Light – central to their metaphysical scheme, and proclaim an existential metaphysics that can be known as gnosis as well as thought. They reject the physicalist reductionism of scientists such as Dawkins and Hawking, as reality is not mono-layered but multi-layered. Through its multiplicity shines the One Being or Light from which all phenomena have come, and in addressing its universal energy, the intuitionists follow the tradition of Bergson, Hulme, Whitehead, William James and Husserl and deny the positivist tradition that reality is solely materialistic or linguistic.

The Fire or Light comes from the beyond, from outside Nature, in rays that are more subtle than gamma rays (and would be found at the gamma end of the electromagnetic spectrum if subtle energies could be recorded on the spectrum), and it enters our porous beings – when we open the channels within our selves and remove the brittle blockages of the dry ego – and fills us like the sea, bringing with it healing properties, wisdom and understanding from the beyond. It can be Providential in lodging knowledge and information that we need without effort on our part, once we have opened to it, and the experience of the Light smoothes out the creases in the psyche and leaves it peaceful, serene, and purified.

This experience of the Fire or Light is universal and happens within all religions. In all cases the mystics have something in common. They have shut down their social ego and opened their soul and spirit or universal being and have seen the Light first as a shimmering in water as it were and then as an intensely bright rising sun. This is an actual experience, not a metaphor.

The Fire or Light, in fact, is the one common ingredient in all cultures, which is found in every region of the world, in North America, in Europe, in Africa, in Asia, and the incidence and importance given to it depends on the youth or age of the civilization in which it is found. It is the common ground of all religions, the ultimate experience that all creeds and dogmas and belief-systems have in common, though some are more aware of it than others. If the creeds and dogmas and religions are like individual trees in a forest, the Light is the common soil in which they are all rooted; and if they are all by individual wells, the Light is the common water-table under the surface, with which they all fundamentally connect. Focus on the local traditions, on the local differences of what is visible above the ground, and the differences between the creeds, dogmas and belief-systems is apparent. Focus on the common deep experience, and the fundamental Oneness of the creeds, dogmas and belief-systems is revealed. I hold that all people's experience of this reality is the same, regardless of where they live or what local creeds they approach it through.

Different local creeds relate to the common experience in different ways, with different emphases as can be seen by revisiting the six possible positions or kinds of religious outlook that individual sects can take towards the common ground (*see* pp44-5), only considering them from a cultural rather than a religious perspective:

1   Adherence to one's local tradition, sect, cult, group or church with no universalism at all. This excludes all other 'trees in the forest'.
2   Emphasis on the universality of the thought of one's local tradition, e.g. evangelical Christianity or Quaker Christianity (with all its credal locality) as the Universalism. This excludes all other traditions.

3   Ecumenism of one's own religion, e.g. Christian ecumenism or Universalist religion under Jesus Christ. This excludes the non-Christian religions.

4   Co-existence between all religions. There is tolerance of all other traditions and religions without convergence.

5   Convergence of faiths while recognizing differences. This accepts a pluralist position while exploring the common ground between all religions and the oneness of the divine mystery of the Fire or Light. All local and regional differences are preserved and the value of diversity is recognized.

6   Syncretism, which is defined by the *Concise Oxford Dictionary* as the 'attempt to unify or reconcile differing schools of thought, sects', and for which there is a spectrum, from attempting to reconcile faiths to achieving a reconciliation of faiths. This sees the divine mystery of the Fire or Light as one and the response as one, and attempts to go beyond diversity to unity. Christian interfaith groups do not like the word syncretism as it can result in a mixture of ingredients taken from all creeds, sects and doctrines at the expense of the purity of each individual local credal tradition, but the Fire or Light is the common ground in which all the differing schools of thought and sects – the trees or wells – are reconciled. Here we are near to a single religion, which many find both unlikely and undesirable.

The interfaith tradition since 1790 reflects the move from Christian Universalism (outlook 3 on my list of six) to convergence-syncretism (outlooks 5 and 6). The American Christian Universalism of George de Benneville in 1741, which has culminated in the Christian Universalism of the World Council of Churches under Jesus Christ, has given way to the convergent-syncretist movement that has stamped its mark inside the UN building itself, where the religious symbol is the pagan Zeus, and which has influenced the many interfaith groups since 1840. At present these interfaith groups emphasize doctrines rather than the Fire or Light, and their growth has kept pace with the growth of the UN, where all religions are to be found, not just Christianity.

Whether we like it or not the world is moving towards globalism and internationalism, and the transnational corporations and satellite media transmissions are two aspects of this. Much of this globalism has come from North America, some of it as a consequence of the space programme, and post-Marshall Plan Europe has followed America's lead. There are moves to create some form of a world government in the 21st century, with the leaders of regional blocs linked by satellite TV, and there is talk of a new world-wide civilization.

A world government has never happened and must therefore be regarded as an aspiration rather than a likelihood. I examined the concept of a world-wide civilization in *The Fire and the Stones*. I see history in terms of civilizations, and in that work I showed that in the past all attempts at world control have come from within a particular civilization and unless we are about to 'break the mould' the same must be true of any coming world-wide civilization, which is in fact a world-wide stage of a particular civilization. I would agree with the conclusion of Samuel Huntington in the summer 1993 issue of the American journal, *Foreign Affairs*: 'There will be no universal civilization, but instead a world of different civilizations, each of which will have to learn to co-exist with the others.' Only I would add that one civilization can persuade all the others to take part in its world-wide stage so that they all appear to belong to a universal or world-wide civilization.

Western civilization is an amalgam of two civilizations and consists of the North American and European civilizations, and I have concluded that a coming world-wide civilization will be a stage (stage 15 out of 61 stages) in the relatively young North American civilization, which is only a quarter of the way through its growth. Even if it seems to be a UN-based civilization, a coming world-wide civilization co-ordinated from the UN would have US power behind it. If it happens, a UN-based world-wide civilization will be a relatively voluntary one in the tradition of the universal Roman Empire – and one inspired by the North American civilization within whose life-cycle it will be a stage.

There are at present two competing scenarios for world government involving different groups. The first has formed round UN-minded internationalist bankers within the North American civilization and comprises a Jewish-American-British-European alliance of the heirs of certain mega-rich dynastic families, the so-called Illuminati who were behind the French Revolution and arguably the American Revolution (through Jefferson) and funded

Communism and Fascism, and whose policies include population-reduction. Its backbone will be the girdle of the Trilateral Commission (North America, Europe and Japan) with all regional blocs (South America, Africa, Asia and others) playing a part. Moves towards this end have long been discussed by the influential so-called advisory groups or pressure groups to the governments of the US and Europe, such as the internationalist American Council on Foreign Relations and the Bilderberg Group. Their deadline for a world government by 2000 has been put back to 2002, and there is concern that it may have to be further postponed.

The second scenario is Pope-led, through the Catholic Church. A new Holy Roman Empire is being created in Europe, a United States of Europe with the Pope as its spiritual head: this is the vision of men such as the Catholic Jacques Delors. After the attempt on his life in May 1981 the Pope apparently (in August 1981) had a vision of a Rome-led world government by the year 2000, one involving a change in Russia, which came about; and with one billion followers, one sixth of humankind, the Pope is the widely acknowledged head of the ecumenical world church (outlook 3) and is well positioned to become spiritual head of a coming world government.

The Fire and the Stones shows that the 'world-wide' stage of a civilization (stage 15 out of 61 stages) is accompanied by a Fire-based change of emphasis in the civilization's orthodox religion, which throws up a heresy that is later grafted on the civilization's orthodox religion. In the Egyptian civilization the heresy involved a shift from Osiris-Re to Amun. In the European civilization the heresy involved a shift from the Catholic Christ to the Protestant Christ (who could be directly approached by supplicants). In the North American civilization I diagnose a change of emphasis in the orthodox religion from the Puritan God of the Pilgrim Fathers to the God/Christ of radical ecumenical Protestantism, and the heresy is a shift to the New Age Universalist God anticipated by the 1776 American Illuminatists such as Jefferson who transformed America after coming under the influence of the French Illuminati. Later on the heresy becomes the orthodoxy when a new people take over a civilization (in stages 26-8): in the Egyptian civilization the New Kingdom, whose god was Amun, and in the European civilization the Renaissance Humanists, whose God was Protestant, not Catholic.

The neo-Illuminati group espouses a heresy, the occultist Light of the New Age's cosmic Christ (Teilhard's UN-based approach).

According to the many books on the subject by detractors, the god of this particular élitist New World Order is Lucifer or Satan and its common ground is money, the billions of dollars the élite can loot from the rest of the world, including South Africa and Russia. This particular heresy can eventually be expected to triumph and be grafted on the orthodoxy, but not until stage 28, and the North American civilization is only in stage 15, which is dominated by orthodoxy, in this case Christianity. Europe's stage 15 ended in 1244, and its heretical renewal came in 1555, 300 years later. So it may be a couple of hundred years at least before the New Age/Illuminati 'heresy' is grafted on the orthodoxy and becomes the new orthodoxy in the North American civilization; until then, the civilization's orthodoxy remains ecumenical Protestantism. The Pope's scenario is actually an attempt to revive the European civilization's 'pre-heresy' vision of Europe (pre-1555), based on the Catholic Light of St Augustine, Pope Gregory and St Bernard, and elevate it into a world-wide stage. This is a very fine Light, but Catholicism is not the North American civilization's orthodoxy.

The European civilization is in a universalist stage but is too far along its parabola – too old in terms of the pattern of civilizations I have found – to create a world government. The European civilization has emerged from a colonial conflict and decolonization (stage 41) and is on the verge of passing into a secularizing conglomerate (stage 43, United States of Europe), while the universalism which has surfaced in stages 15, 28 and 34 surfaces more completely in stage 44. The New Age has had an impact on Europe and there will be some fusion of New Age and Christian ideas, but at this time it will not form a world government within the European civilization. Universalism within the European civilization, and within the Byzantine-Russian, Arab, Indian, Chinese and Japanese civilizations and in Latin America, will make any region that has passed stage 44 susceptible to a unifying approach from the young North American civilization, which is in stage 15.

If there is going to be a universal civilization in the sense of a coming world-wide stage of an existing civilization's orthodoxy (i.e. the North American civilization's), then it is likely to be based on the ideals which triumphed over dictatorship during the Second World War and over totalitarianism during the Cold War: liberal democracy, universal suffrage, freedom and the formation of an alliance between American ecumenical Protestantism and the

Pope's Catholicism – an alliance between America and Europe which would seek the common ground in all civilizations to justify its world-wide stage, the common ground being the Fire or Light. This third way involves ecumenical Protestantism (outlook 2) converging pluralistically with (outlook 5), or even reconciling (outlook 6), the world's religions and the Fire or Light of each, including that of the Jewish Kaballah. Such a third way would be wider and more universal than the way of Christ and it would incorporate elements of the New Age heresy, and it is likely to be a Universalist use of orthodoxy, focusing on the soul of all humankind, the common ground beneath the local traditions, the soil (and water-table) beneath the trees.

Such a third way towards a world-wide stage of a civilization would reflect my philosophy of Universalism, with its emphasis on the Fire or Light. In *The Fire and the Stones* I show that the 'world-wide' stage of a civilization (stage 15) grows round a new Universalist interpretation of the civilization's orthodox central idea of its metaphysical Fire, which in the North American civilization's case will emerge from ecumenical Protestantism. Whatever happens, and whether there is going to be an actual world-wide civilization (in the sense of a world-wide stage in an existing civilization) or not, the 21st century will see increasing globalism and internationalism, and the search for common ground between cultures is going to become more pronounced rather than less pronounced. Political Universalism will develop, encouraging a universal suffrage under which every human being has a vote and is regarded as a world citizen, free from famine, war and genocide. This is an ideal the UN has yet to live up to. Whether it is desirable or not there are bound to be moves towards spiritual Universalism – the perception that all men can make spiritual contact with the Light – and, beyond that, to religious Universalism, the possibility that all men should have the same universal religion. The Fire or Light is crucial to such moves.

I would go so far as to say that a world-wide civilization (albeit a Roman-style stage within the North American civilization) would require a world-wide universal (or Universalist) religion. In the Roman time all local traditions were subordinated to the Roman tradition, and though local individuals continued to worship at their local temple of Isis, Serapis or Zeus, these were identified, either in convergence or syncretistically, with the Universalist Roman religion of Jupiter. In other words, a world-wide civilization based on the UN but controlled behind the scenes by America, would allow all regional differences, the diversity of local sects and creeds, but in identification with the universal religion of the common ground, which could only meaningfully be the Fire or Light within a strong Christian context. What the diverse cultures have in common and what will unite them is their common experience of the Fire or Light throughout the world, in North America, Europe, the Middle East, Tibet, the Far East and Japan. This common ground is far more unitive than the Pope's 'love thy neighbour' Golden Rule, which is an effect of the golden mystic vision: if you know the Fire or Light you instinctively feel love for your neighbour rather than adopt the attitude as a rule. All religions will therefore emphasize what they have in common with other religions, while they practise their own tradition.

I assume growing globalism rather than growing chaos. *The Fire and the Stones* holds that all civilizations go through similar stages, and that through existing civilizations history continues without universal chaos. What is clear is that if globalism is coming, then there needs to be a growing awareness within each religion of its own Tradition of the Fire or Light, the common ground. In some cases there must be a rediscovery of the Fire or Light. There needs to be a Mystic Revival within each religion and across the world, and a Metaphysical Revolution against reductionist science to spread knowledge of this increased awareness of the Fire or Light. Christianity, as the official religion of Western civilization's Christendom, must rediscover its own Fire or Light as an experience independent of doctrine.

Robert Runcie, writing as Archbishop of Canterbury in 1991, said: 'If it can be shown that there is a "common core" or "ultimate sameness" to all religious experience, irrespective of creed, race or society, this could have profound implications for the evolution of common understanding across many of the current barriers which divide people in our world.' *The Fire and the Stones* has shown that the common core or ultimate sameness of all religious experience is the Fire or the Light, and if this can be grasped by Northern and Southern Irish, by Moslems and Jews, by Hindus and Moslems, by Bosnian Christians and Moslems and all warring peoples everywhere, understanding can only be improved. If this understanding can remove famine, war and genocide and result in a universal concord, then it is a good thing that local sects and religions should be aware of their common ground and see truth as one and indivisible as well as partial and diverse, even though the world-wide stage of the North American civilization only lasts for a relatively short time.

REVOLUTION IN THOUGHT AND CULTURE

There was a time in the Middle Ages when European culture was unified and all the disciplines interconnected round a central idea, like branches round a central trunk, the Christian religion, and the whole was fed by a metaphysical sap – 'metaphysical' suggesting a 'Reality beyond the world of physics and Nature', 'beyond the senses', 'energy manifesting into the Universe from beyond it'. In the time of the Crusades European art, literature and music all received the nourishing sap of the metaphysical via the Christian trunk, and there was unity of culture and 'unity of being' (Yeats' phrase). Before the Renaissance the great cultural works of the European civilization's art, sculpture, music, literature and philosophy all expressed a vision (as leaves express sap) of the illumined soul (or halo), which they associated with the examined life, progress to sainthood, serene and ordered Gregorian chantings, stone angels and thought about the divine. It was a vision that made the human condition less grim and bleak, and during the Renaissance Plato-inspired Ficino and Botticelli shared Dante's vision. Despite the Reformation, unity of culture continued during the Elizabethan time and the time of the Metaphysical poets. Since the 18th century, the metaphysical idea expressed through Christianity has dwindled, and our culture has turned secular.

These days we have cultural diversity and multi-culturalism. This is another way of saying that our culture is fractured and fragmented and supplemented by new grafts from ex-colonial territories (Caribbean and Indian). Many would say there is richness in diversity, that the branches of humanistic diversity are preferable to the tree-trunk dictatorship of religion, but the trouble is, diversity of branches with too little metaphysical sap means that the branching out in all directions is brittle and may fall apart. Hardly any of the branches of our culture these days draws on metaphysical vigour. A study could demonstrate in devastating detail the secular nature of the main contemporary works and how little they reflect the metaphysical. Secularization of culture is a consequence of a civilization's decline. And, conversely, a civilization's decline is a consequence of the secularization of culture. A civilization grows through a thrust of metaphysical sap that expresses itself in green-leaf-like culture, and declines when the sap stops and culture turns secular and sere. A metaphysical idea gives every civilization its sap, and civilizations last so long as the sap lasts, so long as it flows and they are renewed, and when the sap fails the civilization declines and its leaf-like culture turns dry and brittle and its branches look bare.

If we think of European culture (our cultural diversity) as our integrated knowledge, beliefs and behaviour – our language, ideas, customs, codes, institutions, rituals, ceremonies, works of art and other intellectual achievements – and if we distinguish 'popular' culture (light entertainment, war films, sport, pop concerts, music, television and the lottery) from 'higher' culture (art exhibitions, concerts, literary events, museums, libraries, bookshops, book reviews, lectures), most of the products of our higher culture in recent times (our art, sculpture, music, literature and philosophy) share attitudes of humanism, secularism, philosophical materialism and scepticism. In other words, the products of our culture share a concern with the human and the mundane, hold that matter is the only reality and that no other vision of Reality is possible; which means there is no God or soul or spirit, and life is a purposeless accident; death is the end, and culture offers perceptions of character in terms of human values – hence Beckett's half-buried figures, Bacon's screaming Popes and shock art at the Royal Academy. Such works express horror at the horror of the humanistic version of the human condition, human interest and warmth, and a diversity of disbelief.

I speak up for the metaphysical idea in our culture, the vision of energy or power which is at the root of our civilization. I do not do so as a committed Christian or as an evangelist or as a hater of humanistic, secular writings; I have the interest in *all* culture of any man of letters, and I am an admirer of the best humanistic works and a devotee of English Literature: Chaucer's *Prologue*, Pope's 'Epistle to Boyle' and Keats' *Odes*. I accept that for many secularization and diversity are irreversible, that the world has moved on (which is another way of saying that our civilization has declined from its metaphysical beginnings and middle). On the other hand, I am worried at how *little* the metaphysical idea is found in our culture. It has become virtually non-existent, the sap is just not reaching the branches at all. I believe there is still room for the metaphysical and that many people derive sustenance from it, that our culture needs a strong metaphysical presence, that the young need to encounter metaphysical works on their largely humanistic, secular courses (works such as 'honey-tongued' Shakespeare's Platonic *Sonnets*, Milton's *Paradise Lost* and Eliot's *Four Quartets*). And it is in this spirit, to correct an imbalance, that I want to start a 'Revolution in thought and culture'. My Revolution is to get some sap moving round the almost dried-up tree to arrest decay.

Besides being a man of letters I am a cultural historian and observer who shares many of Matthew Arnold's views on our culture, which has become further secularized since *Culture and Anarchy* first appeared in 1869. I am cross-disciplinary, and still see our culture as a sap-energized whole even though today it is fragmented, its sapless parts separate. Today there are many specialists, but few cultural historians who are in contact with the vision that reconciles all disciplines, restores the unity of culture and makes a Theory of Everything possible. The poet is allowed to move between disciplines – there are precedents in Matthew Arnold's *Culture and Anarchy*, T E Hulme's *Speculations*, T S Eliot's *Notes Towards the Definition of Culture* and Robert Graves's *White Goddess* – and, claiming such cross-disciplinary licence and looking back to the example of Coleridge, I seek to unify; I look for what is in common between disciplines and different cultures. Specialists analyse and seek differences and make distinctions with rational analysis. I, on the other hand, follow the 'esemplastic power of the imagination' as Coleridge called it (*eis en plattein* – 'shape into one') and unify; help parts that have fallen apart grow back together again, get the sap flowing through the broken branches of our culture so they put out leaves again, and seek to restore the whole view.

That is why I raise the standard of revolt in the name of Tradition. I believe it is the first time in the 20th century that anyone has attempted such a Revolution (or reversal of decay) in so many branches of thought and culture. And how fitting to have raised the banner in the Jubilee Hall, Aldeburgh, where Britten's premières revolutionized British music, and which is as near to the North Sea as it is possible to be. Our march started on the shores of the North Sea, on the outermost margins of our Kingdom, and will continue to Cambridge before culminating in London.[8]

*

Our higher culture is today separated from a long Tradition which used to be central to it, that the highest experience we know is the sublime vision of Reality or vision of God, the vision of Paradise. This reality has traditionally been regarded as being of a higher order than secular, humanistic social life and is independent of the soul or mind that has the vision. It is known in all cultures and civilizations. European painters have tried to capture it: Jan van Eyck's *Adoration of the Lamb*; Fra Angelico's angels in *Christ Glorified in the Court of Heaven* (much used on Christmas cards); and Michelangelo's Sistine Chapel vision. European composers have tried to capture celestial music: in medieval and Renaissance vocal music (notably Gregorian chants); in the sacred choral music of Palestrina, Tallis, Byrd and Monteverdi; and in the Hallelujah chorus of Handel's *Messiah*. European poets have offered it as the goal of man's quest: Dante's sempiternal rose in his *Paradiso*; Milton's 'God is light, … celestial light' in *Paradise Lost* (bk 3); Eliot's 'crowned knot of fire/And the fire and the rose are one' in 'Little Gidding'. Philosophers have seen the brightness in this vision as the source of creation and Nature: Heracleitus's 'ever-living' Fire ('Fragment 30'), Plato's Fire or 'universal Light' which causes the shadows to flicker on the walls of the cave, and Plotinus's 'authentic Light' which 'comes from the One and is the One'. The Fire or Light is what creation manifested from.

This Paradisal vision of Fire or Light can be traced through many cultures where it has glowed at many times during the last 5,000 years, from the Indo-European civilization to ancient Egypt to Mesopotamia, Iran and India, down to the European, and most recently, the North American civilization. The religious teachers refer to it and are identified by it. The Buddha was the Enlightened One, Jesus the Light of the World, Mohammed saw the first page of the Koran written in Fire. The experience is behind Patanjali, the Fire cult of Zoroaster, Mahavira, Lao-Tzu, Mani and George Fox (who founded the Quaker Inner Light). The great European mystics have known it in all cultures: Saint Augustine, Pope Gregory the Great, Bayazid, Al-Hallaj, Omar Khayyam, Suhrawardi, Hafiz, Symeon the New Theologian, St Hildegard of Bingen, Meister Eckhart, Suso, Ruysbroeck, Kempis, Rolle, Hilton, Julian of Norwich, St Catherine of Siena, St Catherine of Genoa, St Teresa of Avila, St Gregory Palamas, Padmasambhava, Sankara, Guru Nanak, Hui-neng, Eisai, Dogen and many others. The vision is to be found as the central idea of many poets: St John of the Cross, Herbert, Vaughan, Crashaw, Traherne, Norris, Law, Marvell, Milton, Blake, Wordsworth, Coleridge, Shelley and in our century, Yeats and Eliot. My own work contains a number of visions of the Fire or Light.

All these people saw the Fire or Light within their soul. They closed their eyes and moved behind their rational, social ego into their universal being and sat and waited, the mystics in contemplation, the poets waiting for images like anglers waiting for fish to bite, and the Fire or Light opened to them like sunlight breaking in water as it did for St Augustine in AD 400 and St Hildegard of Bingen in c1140 (*see* p32). Baroque art symbolized these experiences of illumination in the sunburst, and sunbursts can be seen in Catholic and Protestant churches throughout Europe. The vision of Fire or Light is sometimes described as the vision of God or of Being.

The metaphysical vision of the Fire or the Light (a vision of a divine Reality beyond the world of physics and the senses) is the central idea of the religions of East and West: it is Christian and Orthodox transfiguration, Hindu Yogic samadhi, Mahayana sunyata, the Void of Tao, Buddhist enlightenment and Zen satori. The vision of the Fire or Light expresses itself in a religion and inspires 'stones' (temples, cathedrals or mosques), and the religion then inspires its civilization, for religions inspire civilizations. So Mohammed in his cave saw the Fire which became the first page of the *Koran*, a religion gathered round his vision, and the new Arab culture grew into a civilization as his vision was taken abroad in the time of the Crusades.

In *The Fire and the Stones* I show that the vision of the Fire or Light is the central idea of 25 civilizations and answers the question Toynbee asked, 'What causes the birth of civilizations?'. He never found the answer and wrote in volume 12 of his 12-volume *A Study of History* (which was completed in 1961): 'I have been searching for the positive factor which within the last 5,000 years, has shaken part of Mankind ... into the "differentiation of civilizations" .... These manoeuvres have ended, one after another, in my drawing a blank.' I show that civilizations grow in response to a metaphysical idea (in Europe's case, God as Fire or Light) which is central to their religion, and that they decline when they forget or lose contact with their own central idea and turn secular. A civilization is healthy so long as it continues to reflect its own central idea, its vision of Fire or Light which is recorded in the tradition of its culture, its philosophy, art and literature. (The role of the Fire in history is dealt with very fully in chapters 9 and 10 of *The Fire and the Stones*, and the patterns of the 25 civilizations are in a 7-foot long chart that comes with the book.)

The metaphysical idea is imported into a new civilization from an older civilization, and in the European civilization the Fire or Light was imported from Palestine in the 1st century AD – the vision of Heaven, of Christ and later of the halo – and the European civilization was strong until the 17th century. Its growth stopped about 1914, by which time the European civilization's renewal in the European empires had overextended the civilization and led to internal conflicts and its breakdown in the First World War. The European civilization is now entering a United States of Europe: all its nation-states are undergoing a further process of secularization as part of the European civilization's ongoing decline (though it will be perceived with hope). Western civilization is an amalgam of the European and North American civilizations, and the North American civilization is much younger than the European civilization as writers such as Henry James observed – its Fire or Light was imported from Europe by visionary settlers who established the Jamestown colony (like Bartholomew Gosnold who left Otley Hall, Suffolk to found it in 1607) and by the Pilgrim fathers – and is now in the same stage as the Roman civilization after the two Punic wars, with a world role still to come.

*

The vision of the Fire or Light, which I have described as the highest experience during the growth of the culture (the philosophy, music, art, literature and religion) of a civilization, and which is its central idea, round which it grew, must be revived in every generation if the civilization is to be revitalized and stay alive. The vital, revitalizing sap is released by mystics into the trunk of religion and by philosophers, artists and writers into the civilization's various branches.

Traditionally, the philosophers have contributed to this renewal by interpreting their civilization's central idea of the Fire or Light. In the West, the Church was behind the philosophy of the Middle Ages – Aquinas and the Scholiasts – and at the back of traditional philosophy has been metaphysics, a branch of philosophy. Having started as the 'philosophy *after* physics' (Aristotle's *ta meta ta phusika*) and having become 'the study of the first principles of things, including such concepts as being, substance, essence, time, space, cause, identity' or 'the ultimate science of Being and Knowing' (OED), metaphysics came to focus on what is *beyond* physics, or what is *behind* or *hidden within*, physics; what E W F Tomlin called 'the concealed Absolute'. Metaphysics became the science of a universal Whole, concerned with 'the endeavour to frame a coherent, logical, necessary scheme of general ideas in terms of which every element of our experience can be interpreted' (Whitehead, *Process and Reality*, 1929), and in the course of offering a metaphysical scheme, philosophers touched on and renewed their civilization's central idea for their generation.

Metaphysics approaches the structure of Reality, which is 'beyond or behind the physical' (the invisible behind the visible, the infinite behind the finite) through ontology (the study of Supreme Being or Reality), transpersonal or spiritual psychology (the study of the location of the part of the self that knows Being), epistemology (the study of how Being is known) and cosmology (the study of the structure of the Universe). Traditionally, ontology did not have a materialistic, sceptical sense, nor did it refer to the reality of the phenomenal world; rather it was the study of Being, which is both transcendent and immanent, the transcendent Fire that is beyond the Universe (as Creator) and immanent Light manifested within the Universe (as the Fire's expression of itself within Nature). So long as they kept transcendence and immanence as their subject matter, European metaphysical philosophers were very close to the central idea of the European civilization and kept it alive.

However, since the Renaissance, European philosophers have in varying degrees been linked with humanist movements which have secularized the European civilization and taken it away from its central idea by means of Rationalism (Kant and Descartes),

Scepticism (Hume), Empiricism (Locke) and Materialism (Hobbes among others). In other words, the humanist movements claim that one can only know what one's reason and sense data tell one, and that there is nothing to be known beyond matter, no vision of Reality. Speculative reason and logic from Leibniz and Kant onwards made metaphysics more and more speculative and caused the metaphysical vision of Plato and others to sink into disrepute. Since Newton philosophers have progressively weakened the function of the metaphysical idea in the European civilization; and as Christianity has become increasingly weak since c1870, so the European civilization has declined further from its central vision into secularization, humanism, Rationalism, scepticism, Empiricism, materialism, mechanism and positivism (being concerned with the world, human affairs, the reason, doubt, the senses, mechanical explanations, observable facts). Nevertheless, philosophy remains the study of the structure of Being, which can be known in the vision that is central to philosophers, mystics and poets and which is the central idea of the civilizations of history.

This Tradition of a vision of Reality has shown partial signs of a revival in the 20th century through discoveries in science. Following the First Scientific Revolution of Galileo and Newton, a Second Scientific Revolution began in 1905 with Einstein, relativity and quantum mechanics and post-war subatomic physics, which led to the Third Scientific Revolution in cosmology in the 1980s (which combined relativity and quantum theories). Twentieth-century science has undermined traditional science by using the mathematics of Einstein's relativity theory and Heisenberg's quantum theory. The traditional 17th century science of Newton was based on observation, sense data, experiment and testing and produced classical physics and reductionism, which describes a whole in terms of its parts (i.e. it analyses) and assumes that mind is mere brain function and that the Universe is granular, materialistic and mechanistic; that only the objective phenomenal world is real and that its reality can only be apprehended through positivist observation and sense data by a scientist who is separate from the world he is studying. The 19th century granular world of matter has been replaced by a sea of energies in which light can be both particles and waves, and electrons have uncertain positions and are events in a process.

Now the objective phenomenal world is subject to invisible

underlying quantum forces, and observation and sense data are subject to the mathematics of an observer who is part of the Universe he is observing. (Paradoxically Newton, having established classical physics, spent 30 years looking for an expanding force in light which counterbalances gravity, and never found it, as I describe in my poem 'Against Materialism'.) The revolution in physics has reinforced the perception of the mystics and the perennial wisdom, as books like Capra's *Tao of Physics* have shown, and it has brought back the notion of an invisible, metaphysical force in our time. Einstein said, 'Anyone who studies physics long enough is inevitably led to metaphysics.' In the West there has been a resurgence of interest in the spirit and meditation at the expense of traditional Western religion – interest in man seen as a unity, as a spirit manifesting into body, all one, and not a dualism of soul and inconvenient body. This renewed interest has amounted to a religious revolution, and there has been a parallel revolution in medicine, with a rise in alternative medicine and interest in healing energies pouring into healers.

Philosophy was influenced by the physics of 1905, which found its way into the work of Bergson (the philosopher of Vitalism) and Whitehead. Philosophers have always put forward models of reality – Plato, Leibniz and Kant in particular put forward theoretical and speculative metaphysical models – and William James, Bergson, T E Hulme (in his Bergsonian phase), Whitehead (who was influenced by Bergson's 'process philosophy' and *élan vital*) and Husserl were poised to carry this approach forward around 1910. Unfortunately, the humanistic Vienna Circle took over. Logical Positivism and linguistic analysis saw reality as granular, phenomenal and observable and insisted it could be described in language. The Vienna Circle disqualified metaphysics. Its philosophers insisted on a verification principle which could test metaphysical principles by observation and sense data, and they attacked the language of metaphysics, saying one cannot ask, 'What is the meaning of life?' because the question is meaningless. But it isn't. In the 20th century, first Russell, then early Wittgenstein and Ayer half-snapped philosophy from its trunk. Existentialism (Marcel excepted), the reaction against linguistic analysis, tore philosophy further from its metaphysical roots by identifying with the rational, social ego's choices in the visible finite world rather than with the soul or transcendental ego or universal being or essence which can glimpse metaphysical Reality in the invisible infinite world. Structuralism and its offshoots or sub-branches did further damage. Derrida holds, *Il n'y a rien hors du texte*: There is no reality outside the text. That is wrong. Reality, the Fire or Light, is known in a vision beyond language.

*

The return of metaphysics after 1905 has been only partial, then, and despite the two revolutions in physics, it has run into opposition from philosophy. There has been no challenge to humanism, Rationalism, Empiricism and scepticism (giving primacy to human affairs, the reason, the senses and doubting), although Husserl's phenomenology and Heidegger have made chinks. Scepticism and concerns with language still rule philosophy.

In *The Universe and the Light* I challenged humanism with the philosophy of Universalism, a new philosophy of the 1990s that approaches metaphysical Reality. Universalism, a restatement of metaphysics, is a science that states the Universe in terms of metaphysical Supreme Being or Fire or Light (metaphysical ontology), which manifests into the structure of the Universe and Nature (cosmology) and whose universal energy can be known by the universal self or being or soul-spirit (transpersonal psychology and epistemology). Knowing the Fire or Light requires a transformational shift from the rational, social ego to the deeper universal part of the self, on which Universalist transpersonal psychology reports.

Universalist ontology and cosmology trace how the structure of our Universe has manifested from the Fire or Light, through a Form from Movement process. In this process, the *moving*, infinite first principle, the metaphysical, self-entangled energy of the Fire or Nothingness, is limited into a regular movement and spiral (Non-Being), and out of the pressure of the infinite Fire on the spiral come two pre-particles, one of which is annihilated, leaving the other as an empty vacuum or point or singularity (Being). Out of this point, Existence – Form – manifests as energy becoming matter through the Big Bang in accordance with Einstein's equation, the expanding Universe of the countless trillions of stars which Hubble discovered.

The continuing manifestation from moving Nothingness to Existence is a perpetual process, and is happening all the time, right now, and metaphysical Light constantly manifests into natural light. The Universalist Reality, the Fire or Light, controls the Universe and makes a Theory of Everything possible by including the missing principle of the Fire or Light's (purposive) involvement in creation *before the Big Bang* (or hot beginning), without which there can be no Theory of Everything. (Physics-based cosmology begins *after the Big Bang*, and regards creation as an accident, and will never be able to explain what is essentially metaphysical.) A Universalist Theory of Everything begins with the metaphysical Fire, and my mathematical formula for a Theory of Everything that encompasses the origin and creation of the Universe (my Form from Movement Theory) is: $M \rightarrow M\text{-}S + S$. In S, $+p + \text{-}p = 0$. In S, $+p \rightarrow B$, which evolves $I_1, I_2, I_3...I_n$. $B \rightarrow E$, which is I_{n+1}. (M=movement; S=spiral; p=particle; B=Being; I=implicate order; E=Existence. Details are in *The Universe and the Light*.)

Another way of putting it is to say that the visible Universe – Nature and matter – has manifested like shadows from the Light. I ended one of my first poems and also one of my most recent poems, nearly 40 years later, with the same line: 'Behind each shadow reigns a glorious sun.' Universalism sees the sun behind each manifestation of the phenomenal world, and it is therefore in the tradition of Plato.

In its ontology and cosmology (structure of Being) Universalism proposes a metaphysical science. Bergson (in his *Introduction to Metaphysics*, 1903, two years before Einstein's 1905 paper) called for a 'much-desired union of science and metaphysics', and Universalism provides this union by combining Bergson's *élan vital* as Light, Einstein's relativity theory, quantum theory and the metaphysical manifestation from the Fire or Light into the cosmology of a Universalist Universe. Universalism states a universal (Universe-wide) ordered metaphysical Whole or cosmos, or One or All which has control over its parts, radiating from the source of the Universe to all humankind and all creatures the invisible, hidden, unphysical, metaphysical universal energy of the Fire or Light along with invisible Fire-produced Dark Matter, which passes through our bodies and fills 99 per cent of the Universe (the apparently empty part), and every room. The One radiates from Non-Being into the universal being and existence of all organisms with great universality, and is an organizing force that manifests from beyond Nature into Nature, the Universe, and drives organisms forward into ever higher unities within the overall unity, towards a universal, non-physical purpose. Universalism's universal force is the drive behind evolution and the rise of consciousness, which brains transmit: mind is not dependent on brain but enters brain, which is transmissive.

In its panoramic sweep Manifestational Universalism focuses on 'all existing things', the whole creation and *all* energies – paranormal, supernatural, mystical as well as physical – that humankind can open to as well as their structure. It includes every possible concept of the mind; not every *existing* concept but every *possible* concept, which includes things abstract or concrete, natural or supernatural, known or unknown, probable or improbable, physical or metaphysical. The most fundamental concept of metaphysics is the idea that encompasses a universal All – infinity, in an infinite number of dimensions including those we know, i.e. infinite space (endless space without beginning or end) and infinite time (eternity without beginning or end). Universalism is not holism, which is concerned with the *physical* whole in space and the world of physics and hierarchies of biological organism. (It is possible to be holistic and physicalist and not metaphysical at all.) Universalism is therefore to be contrasted with reductionism and holism, which are two sides of the same physicalist coin and emphasize the parts and the whole.

In its psychology and epistemology (which investigate how Reality is known), Universalism is an existential contemplative philosophy as well as a science, and the Universalist manifesting Reality, the Fire or Light, can be known existentially in the mystic vision, which can be achieved by contemplation. Universalism is therefore in part a development of Vitalism and Existentialism. Experiences of the Fire or Light are received in consciousness where they are studied by the phenomenological technique of 'bracketing out' their source. By bracketing out the *source* of the Fire or Light we can make a 'self-report' on its *appearance* in consciousness which has a quasi-empirical status and is a valid subject for scientific and philosophical inquiry. Such an approach proposes a new view of man along with its new view of the Universe. Like light, man can be both a particle and a wave. In a Universe which is full of invisible energies that flow into it and through it, human consciousness can be both a particle (a social ego, a brain like a dry sponge) and a wave (a porous sponge-like universal self through which pours the sea of energies of 20th-century science). I tried to capture contemplation within the sea of energies in the fifth stanza of my poem 'A Metaphysical in Marvell's Garden' (*see* pp140-1).

A person can open to the universal energy of the Fire or Light which radiates into the Universe and one's universal being or self, bringing powers of infused wisdom and knowledge (as the mystic Tradition recounts). Universalism focuses on the soul's opening to the Light in mystic illumination, when sweetness forms on the soul like morning dew, and sees experience as a quest in which the soul existentially confronts the Light (or immanent God). Such a view gives meaning to Whitehead's words at the end of *Modes of Thought* (1938): 'The purpose of philosophy is to rationalize mysticism.' What does one have to do to be a contemplative Universalist? One has to make an effort to become a Seeker and quest for Truth and know the universal energy of the Fire or Light through inner contemplation. Such an experience reveals the Universe as it really is and gives a correct view of the limited power of reason, logic, the senses, matter and social, human affairs as the spirit, lit by the Light from within, knows that it is immortal (as Wordsworth knew in his Ode, 'Intimations of Immortality') and that there is a Reality beyond the physical world.

This new philosophy challenges humanism and its assumption that this life is all, that death is the end and that there is no Truth to quest to, no vision or purpose to find, (that one must just sit back and be futile with a passive mind in the sense of not using its esemplastic or whole-making powers). It echoes Coleridge's questioning of humanism and scientific materialism when he wrote of the Newton of the 1660s (as opposed to the questing Newton of the next 30 years): 'Newton was a mere materialist – *Mind* in his system is always passive – a lazy looker-on on an external World .... Any system built on the passiveness of the mind must be false as a system' (*Collected Letters II*, p709). The Universalist admires all the human virtues but sees humanism as a lazy option that avoids the need to become a Seeker and quest towards Reality, to use the esemplastic or whole-making powers of the mind, to approach the vision which holds the meaning of life. The new philosophy therefore challenges reductionism's view that mind can be reduced to mere brain function. It debunks Rationalism, Empiricism and Scepticism (seeing the reason, the senses and doubt as being the foundation for certainty in knowledge), and it demolishes logical positivism and linguistic analysis, for it offers the traditional Reality of philosophy and shows that it can be known by gnosis through meditation and contemplation.

Reality is outside and independent of language, and Universalism bypasses the Vienna Circle's verification process and its focus on language by offering hundreds of reports of the experience of Reality, of the Fire or Light, which are received in the intellect as opposed to the reason. Intellect, Latin *intellectus*, meaning 'inner perception or understanding' as in the 'intellectual vision' (of the Light) in Shelley's 'Hymn to Intellectual Beauty', is the faculty that approaches Truth through the 'eye of contemplation' (St Bonaventure) as opposed to the 'eye of the flesh', the corporeal eye of the physical body that is one of the five senses, or 'the eye of reason' which sees philosophical categories and organizes sense data. Reason, rational inquiry, and sense data are useful instruments as far as they go, but the wise know that they only take the Seeker so far, after which only the contemplative 'intellect' can take him on to his destination. This is known in the Zen temples, where they close down the reason and the senses so that the intellect or inner perception can open in satori to the Light of Reality. Universalism restores the intellectual vision of the One to primacy, the 'ever-living Fire' of Heracleitus, the Reality Plato and Plotinus knew, which has lurked behind philosophy ever since the Greek philosophers.

It is no longer possible for philosophy and science to go on operating along reductionist lines – there can be no Theory of Everything out of reductionism or physicalist holism. A Theory of Everything must cover *before* as well as *after* the Big Bang and include the moving Fire of metaphysics; and it is not desirable for philosophers and scientists to take a gradual step forward in the direction of physicalist holism, for such gradualism will not fundamentally change anything. In philosophy and science, there is a need for a sudden and abrupt change that involves a radical break with the past, a Revolution that will sweep away reductionism and related false theories such as analytic and linguistic philosophy, logical atomism, logical positivism, linguistic analysis, structuralism, deconstruction and post-structuralism, which have confined reality to language and text. The Revolution will restore the Reality of the Tradition to all disciplines, and put them in harmony with the revolution in physics, the return of the spirit in world religions and the new paradigm in alternative medicine.

Philosophy can return to the position it was in c1910 at the time of William James, Bergson, T E Hulme, Whitehead and Husserl. Once again an invisible, infinite, manifesting Reality can dominate contemporary philosophy. Philosophers must again look outwards at the Universe and consider the evidence of telescopes, instead of sitting in their armchairs and logic-chopping over meanings. They must again seek the unity in the structure of Being – the Whole – rather than analyse and reduce to parts and work in fragments, and central to their unifying is the Universalist vision of Reality as Fire or Light, which marries cosmology and metaphysical cosmology, physics and the philosophical view of the cosmos, physical holism and mysticism, and science and metaphysics into a coherent Whole. Universalism gets behind all difference and conflict to the unity behind diversity – in culture, philosophy, religion, history and literature the coherent Whole of Universalism gets behind diversity.

*

The movement away from metaphysics in philosophy since 1910, away from the Universe to concepts, has had an effect on history. Just as analytical philosophers have directed attention away from the Universe to the concepts of the philosophers who attempt to describe the Universe, so analytical philosophers of history (such as Dilthey, Croce, Collingwood and Vico), influenced by philosophy, have directed attention away from past events, 'speculative' pattern and the identification of civilizations to the categories and concepts of historians. Postmodernists have denied that the past can be objectively studied and that the truth about historical action can be uncovered.

The Universalist Revolution is reversing all that. Just as it has reinstated the vision of Reality in philosophy, Universalism has also reinstated the vision of Reality within the totality of history. Universalism holds that civilizations do not have their genesis in economic or military or political causes. The vision of the Fire or Light, which I have shown in *The Fire and the Stones* was the vision that has grown 25 civilizations, is received by mystics, not economists or generals. The Truth-statements of the key Seekers and mystics are crucial to the establishment of civilizations, just as the renewal of the vision by Seekers and mystics, philosophers and artists is crucial to the development of civilizations.

Just as the Fire or Light is responsible for a civilization's growth, so the absence of the vision is responsible for its decline. There is therefore a link between the decline of the European civilization and the absence of the Light. The Seeker (who becomes a mystic) is the spearhead of a civilization at all times. During the European civilization's growth, the Seeker went into the Church. During its decline, the Seeker becomes aware of himself as living in a rubbishy culture and civilization. ('What are the roots that clutch, what branches grow/Out of this stony rubbish?' Eliot asks in 'The Waste Land'.) Seeking through his misery, he grasps the significance of living by the Light, his higher purpose. (That is the theme of my long poem 'The Silence', which was written in 1964-6.) Once enlightened, the Seeker becomes a mystic, and he can then contribute to the salvation of his culture and civilization by renewing the vision of growth, which counters secular humanism. When Seekers cease to be enlightened in great numbers, they lose their aim and purpose, and the civilization which they lead also loses its aim and declines. The few Seekers who are enlightened are then in the position of revolutionaries. When a civilization loses its control, the Seekers and men of genius think in materialistic, humanistic categories instead of spiritual categories. A civilization declines when spirit is swamped by matter and it loses its belief in its own central idea, turning instead to scepticism. A civilization recovers control when its leaders (the Seekers) return to the spiritual life, and that means returning to the contemplative life. A civilization recovers control when enlightened Seekers form a revolutionary movement in a time of decline.

Universalist history is global in outlook. Its field is not nation-state 'slices of history' (reductionist parts) but the universal Whole in its Universalist sense, the metaphysical Whole or One or All. There was a time when all Christendom was the proper subject of history, and James I was deemed 'the wisest fool in Christendom' (by Henri IV of France and his Minister Sully). Except for Bossuet in his *Discours sur L'Histoire Universelle* (1681) and then Toynbee, historians have become more specialized and partial, focusing on a part of one country's or a continent's history. A child of the sceptical, rational Enlightenment, Gibbon focused on Rome (1766-88) and got the Byzantine civilization wrong. He saw it as a continuation of the West Roman Empire – and could not understand why it expanded under Justinian – rather than as a new civilization with an Orthodox religion that passed into the Russian civilization after the fall of Constantinople in 1453. Spengler's *Decline of the West* was Euro-centric. Before the 1980s only Toynbee focused on all civilizations, and he made fundamental mistakes. (For example he saw the Byzantine civilization as being continued by the Ottomans who had a totally different religion, the Moslem religion, for its metaphysic). In his cyclical *A Study of History* (1934-61), Toynbee made a valiant attempt to understand all history, but he left metaphysics out of the genesis and growth of civilizations and missed the importance of the metaphysical vision, which is not often studied by historians. The motive force of civilizations is a vision (the vision of Reality), and it can only be found by a cross-disciplinary approach, by looking outside history's compartment.

In history, too, there is a need for an abrupt change. The coming global unity which is scheduled for 2002 (and with it the United States of Europe, which is already a reality – with plans for a single currency moving ahead – and is intended as a stepping-stone to a world government) means that it is no longer possible for history to operate on the old nation-state basis (reductionist parts), and history can no longer avoid asking the right questions such as 'What is the unit of world history?' (answer, 'the civilization') and 'What causes the genesis and growth of civilizations?' (answer, 'the vision of Fire or Light'). There must be a fundamental change in history's perspective, and this will produce a new kind of history, whose foundations I have laid in *The Fire and the Stones*. Historians must look outwards at the totality of history in the Universe and must again see history as a whole and not in small pieces, parts, fragments; and central to the totality of history is the metaphysical Whole and the vision of Reality as Fire or Light.

*

The dead-end philosophy reached after 1910 has had an effect on European literature, which after Pound, Eliot and Yeats has been concerned with the phenomenal world and the social ego. The scepticism and materialistic cosmology of modern philosophy has resulted in sceptical, reductionist scientists such as Hawking filling the void left by philosophy and influencing literature. Hawking says we have no special place in the Universe, as first the earth, then the sun have been dethroned from being its centre. (As Hubble has discovered there is no centre to the Universe, which is expanding and inflating like a balloon, while the chemistry of our bodies is the same as the chemistry of the stars, suggesting we are just stardust.) I, on the other hand, hold that as everything began in one point and the metaphysical source of that point, the moving Fire, radiates into us, we have a very special place in the Universe. Neo-Darwinists claim that we live in a purposeless Universe – indeed, that as a result of the Second Law of Thermodynamics, everything is running down and we are living on a 'dunghill of purposeless interconnected corruption' – which is the view of Beckett's characters. In Sartre, Camus, Kafka, Beckett, Hemingway and Orwell, the phenomenal world is all and man is a defeated, purposeless, 'useless passion' (Sartre) who lives under the 'benign indifference of the Universe' (Camus) or the political reality of a regional branch of world government (Orwell's Big Brother), unable to attain the Castle which he seeks (Kafka) and which, despite its hint of metaphor, is set in an uneasy phenomenal world. Some writers like Greene and Waugh are concerned with social Christian dogma, and many novelists convey a social view of characters without suggesting the new perception of man and its possibilities.

Very few writers have reflected the new view of reality in literature. Eliot attempted to absorb it in his *Four Quartets*, Durrell reflected it in the structure of his *Alexandrian Quartet* (in which the four books are supposed to represent three dimensions of space and one of time) and C P Snow called for writers to acquire more knowledge of science, something that has manifestly failed to happen in a way that is fundamental to their work and their view of Reality (as opposed to influencing a technique or gimmick). For the world of most contemporary writers is still granular and materialistic and blind to a new model of reality. It is simply not good enough that the great majority of novelists, dramatists and poets are setting their works in the phenomenal world alone, writing about social egos and relationships and making partial statements that ignore the Whole and amount to endorsements of mind-body humanism (which discounts soul, spirit, and an after-life), Rationalism, Empiricism, reductionism, materialism, mechanism, scepticism, positivism (giving primacy to the reason, sense data, parts, matter, mechanical explanations, doubt and observable facts) – in sum, the false views that have dogged the 20th century and have contributed to the huge wastage of human life in wars and similar disasters.

The new Universalist view of man restores all his traditional powers which the false views have eroded. In the Middle Ages, man was body, mind, soul and spirit, operating within a dualistic Christianity that frowned on and subjugated the body. The revolution that we know as the Renaissance shifted the focus to the body and mind from the soul and spirit, which were marginalized along with the halo, the illumined vision of the spirit, and then largely eliminated from art. Representing the phenomenal world alone was the business of the artist, even though he still drew on Christian stories, parables and themes. The Romantic revolution, among other things, focused on feelings at the expense of the reason and restored the metaphysical perspective of contact with the 'Wisdom and Spirit of the Universe' (Wordsworth), with an 'unseen power' (Shelley). The Modernist revolution turned against post-Romantic, Georgian feeling for the countryside and dwelt on the agony of cultural fragmentation following the wreckage of Europe in the First World War, in which nothing made sense. Man became an alienated, shocked, purposeless, futile creature who could connect 'nothing with nothing' (Eliot). Since then there have been minor movements (such as The Movement in English Poetry in 1956, which was anti-Romantic and neo-Classical and insisted on poems being rational statements set in social situations). Now the new Universalist view of man and the Universe restores human immortality. Man is an invisible body within a visible body, infinite within his finite envelope, and this spiritual body can survive death – that is what reports of the near-death experience tell us. Man is again a body, mind, soul and spirit, and it is the soul-spirit which channels the universal energy of the Fire or Light, and knows the Reality of philosophy in the post-Existentialist Universalist gnosis (or knowing).

A Universalist Revolution is essential in literature. A fundamental, sudden and abrupt change needs to take place, and must be called for. The phenomenal world is not the only reality. Man is not merely body and mind, he has immortality. Novels need to include a dimension of the universal, metaphysical Whole, the One, behind their focus on narrative relationships and character in parts of the Whole (reductionist parts). So do plays (as Shakespeare's did, for example the reference to 'the lark at heaven's gate' in *Cymbeline*) and so do poems. So do painting and music. Some of the outstanding English literature from Chaucer to Pope and Jane Austen has contained sharp social observation, focusing on character defects and espousing the human virtues of kindness, tolerance, mercy, decency and consideration and care for one's fellow human beings, all of which are in harmony with the infinite Whole and are much admired by metaphysical philosophers. Some of the different genres in literature (e.g. the dramatic monologue, narrative verse) usually require exclusively secular treatment. Nonetheless the spectrum of differing genres reserves a central place for Truth-bearing contemplative-reflective odes in secular settings, and for the sublime vision. Like the greatest philosophy and art, the greatest literature reflects the writer's highest perceptions of Reality and of the Age, and leads readers forward to Truth. The greatest literature is Truth-bearing.

The Universalist Revolution bears the metaphysical Fire or Light within social settings in literature and combines sense and spirit – the phenomenal world of the senses and the spiritual beyond – as they were combined in Baroque art, which showed both dynamic movement in the world (often symbolized by wind) and the world of spirit (often symbolized by clouds). (I think of Bernini's sensuously sculpted, swooning, mystic St Teresa.) The new Universalist literature is taking its place alongside existing humanistic secular literature and the Universalist Revolution in literature follows the Baroque and is *neo-Baroque* in mixing the metaphysical and the secular. Just as the Baroque threw up epic (Milton's *Paradise Lost*), a mixture of metaphysical and secular, so has neo-Baroque. My *Overlord*, a poetic epic on the struggle between Eisenhower and Hitler at the end of the last war at the secular level, and on the struggle between Heaven and Hell for differing New World Orders on earth at the metaphysical level, is an attempt at a Universalist epic: a latter-day Sistine chapel vision of the metaphysical world's involvement in secular manoeuvres for war and peace. Epic requires a metaphysical-secular culture in which all can find common ground, and I have produced my epic because I have been to the past and revisited the common ground of metaphysical belief which allows a panoramic sweep of the Whole. I am not impressed when secular critics who are self-confessedly anti-metaphysical say that epic is impossible today because there is no common ground of belief or common culture. (Of course there isn't, if the metaphysical is rejected in favour of total secularism. Of course there isn't, if the past and the

Whole are ignored.)

A Revolution is happening in subject matter and technique (i.e. there is a new concern with metaphysical Reality) as the neo-Baroque style mixes Classicism and Romanticism and combines traditional and organic form, statement and image: Classical statement in social situations in traditional form, and fresh Romantic image and mystic vision in organic form. Universalist poems are about the Quest, illumination, glimpses of Reality, and their soaring vision is grounded in a return from rhymeless rhythm or free verse to rhyme and metre. Universalist verse plays show man's aspirations in relation to the One Reality behind the Universe. Universalist stories contain revelations of Being. Kingsley Amis wrote in the first Movement anthology *New Lines* (1956), 'Nobody wants any more poems on the grander themes for a few years.' In a lean time of sharp and ironic ordinariness in literature, the Universalist Revolution is bringing back the sap that produces grander, loftier themes (which Wordsworth knew) along with the new view of man and the Universe that amounts to a new or Second Renaissance.

Traditionally philosophy, history and literature were branches on one unified tree-trunk, religion, and were permeated by the sap of a metaphysical vision which was central to religion and the arts alike. In a unified, rather than a fragmented culture – in a growing rather than a declining civilization, or in a reviving phase of a declining civilization – this is the case: philosophy, history and literature are all sap-fed branches from one trunk, religion, as they were in the Europe of the Middle Ages. Today, following vandalistic shakings since Newton, the sap has dried up and the brittle branches are almost severed from their trunk.

*

Today the whole of our European culture is fractured at both the popular and higher levels and is in deep malaise. Practitioners in the arts today are separated from the metaphysical energy which thrust their civilization into being, and so they are impoverished, rootless. In *Culture and Anarchy* Matthew Arnold defines culture as the 'study of perfection', of the works of the 'best self', which he says are of 'like spirit with poetry', that which Swift in his *Battle of the Books* called 'sweetness and light' – that which is achieved by '*euphuia*', the finely tempered nature that looks beyond bodily activities and seeks to nourish the soul. Culture involves the pursuit of perfection (an 'inward condition of the mind and spirit') by getting to know 'the best which has been thought and said in the world'. I would say culture is the best aspirations of the human spirit within a civilization, as expressed in the arts and architecture, and that it has transmitted knowledge from past generations to our generation and will pass knowledge on from our generation to future generations.

The 'most perfect' works of our time have nothing in common save humanism and scepticism (i.e. their focus on human life and doubt). Our higher culture is not bearing the fruit it should be bearing. It has secular leaves and shrivelled metaphysical fruit because its sap has ceased to flow from its roots in the One, the metaphysical vigour which in the Middle Ages found expression in the illumined vision of the Church. Landscapes (like Constable's) which show the serenity, unity, composure and tranquillity of Nature, have been replaced by disjointed abstract art. Spatial art, atonal music and doodle poems represent a huge decline in quality in relation to Michelangelo, Beethoven and Dante. The secular works being produced often invite the question: 'So what?' A memory – so what, unless it points us to Truth? The pervasiveness of popular culture has meant that many higher culture novels and poems have the same humanistic, secular outlook on the world as *Mrs Dale's Diary* or *The Archers*, at a more sophisticated and subtle level of character and language, no doubt, but still at their end of the spectrum. At the secular level, such works may be entertaining – in poetry they may lead to phrases of praise such as 'cool syntactical windings', 'concision', 'tactile sonorities', 'clever glooms and charmed lightenings' or 'self-deprecatingly funny', 'salvaging beauty from squalor' or 'wonderfully sardonic and ironic' and in novels 'full of linguistic inventiveness', 'creates an authentic narrative voice', 'well-observed', 'keeps one's attention' – but in relation to the principles of the highest or profoundest art they are simply below the standard of the best, a shallow 'dumbing down' from the high vision of the Tradition.

We now live in a fractured culture in which anything goes: performance takes the place of substance, PR gimmicks and sensationalist 'shock art' crowd out classical painting, music and literature. Standards have collapsed and no one is sure of what is good any more. Conveying Truth is now less important than capturing attention. To improve their own ratings newspapers and the media pitch their articles and programmes at the greatest number of potential 'consumers', who are sometimes deemed to be more interested in a review of a book on Elvis than in one on Reality. (Eliot wrote, 'Humankind cannot bear very much reality.') Our fractured culture is one in which bemused, sceptical people who are unsure of their own beliefs or believe nothing occupy key positions within the Establishment and, unsure of what to do, find it safe to stick with the secular and ignore those whose work challenges the received 'wisdom' of scepticism, and so keep the secular sceptics in business and advance our culture's terminal decay. Presiding over the British scene is a Ministry for Culture, Media and Sport, the linkage of which evidently regards our higher culture as being on a par with secular, popular media and sport.

The Universalist Revolution in modern thought – in philosophy, history and literature and other disciplines such as the sciences and art – can heal the malaise in our culture for it is actually a counter-Revolution which restores the Tradition that we have forgotten, which is the central idea of European civilization; and if enough practitioners join the Revolution and convey its sap, their revival of the European vision will revitalize and reunify our now desiccated and brittle European culture. A group of Universalist thinkers, writers, artists, painters, sculptors and composers can act as a kind of latter-day Pre-Raphaelite Group and recreate philosophy, history, literature, art and music round European civilization's traditional central metaphysical energy, and so reunify Europe's culture at a higher level. Each renewal of a declining civilization's central idea revives that civilization as sap revitalizes dry and brittle branches, and so it is desirable that Europe's current secularization should be arrested by such a metaphysical movement for cultural renewal.

There would be one central idea in the work of such a Group: the metaphysical vision of the Fire or Light, which all would reflect in their work. This idea would draw sustenance from the deepest roots of European culture by renewing the European metaphysical vision as it was when it was strong and there was growth in the European civilization. Just as the 19th-century Pre-Raphaelite artists themselves (Holman Hunt, Millais and Dante Gabriel Rossetti) sought to emulate the work of Italian artists before the time of

Raphael, so the Group I envisage would be a pre-Rationalist Group to emulate the unified art of the Middle Ages, Renaissance and Baroque before the Age of Reason split European culture into reason and (later) feeling, and developed scientific materialism from Newton's discoveries. It would anyway be a pre-Vienna Circle Group that would be a pro-Einstein-and-Vitalist Group.

In calling for the metaphysical to exist alongside the secular through such a Group, I am not siding with Christianity against the art of the Renaissance or of Greek Hellenism before it (which Arnold distinguished from Christian 'Hebraism'); I seek to renew the metaphysical idea within Greek Hellenism and the Renaissance. The Greek art of Pheidias perfectly captured the Greek metaphysical central idea, the serene divinity of Zeus, in his statue at Olympia which was one of the seven wonders of the ancient world, and the artists of the Renaissance – Giotto, Leonardo, Michelangelo – are all imbued with the metaphysical idea. In both Greek and Renaissance artists beauty, harmony and inner and outer human perfection have been expressed with the highest and most perfect skill. Far from calling for metaphysical Hebraism to be admitted to a secular Hellenistic dictatorship, I am lamenting the fact that modern Hellenism has lost contact with its own metaphysical roots which Pheidias exemplified, and I am seeking to help it make a reconnection by paving the way.

A latter-day Pre-Raphaelite Group can rediscover a common cultural vitality by returning to the past. As all civilizations grow from the same metaphysical vision, in a healthy civilization and culture (in Europe's case until 1660) there is a core of belief around that vision which is vital, and cultural vitality is reflected in creative vitality – the relationship between cultural vitality and creative vitality is very close – and poets and philosophers, artists and scientists all have common ground and creative vitality in the culture of the civilization's vital central idea. As I have said, Dante, Ficino and Botticelli all share a vision. In an unhealthy civilization and culture (in Europe's case after 1660, but especially after 1910) there is no central essence of belief associated with the vision that inspired its growth, and consequently there is no cultural vitality in relation to a metaphysical idea, only humanistic diversity. Without cultural vitality to nourish him, the artist-Seeker, must go back to the past and rediscover his roots in the cultural vitality of the past, which is then reflected in his own newly discovered creative vitality.

The artist needs to derive his creative vitality by rediscovering his roots in the civilization's and culture's metaphysical idea, and he draws fragments of this idea into his work, as did the poets of 1910-20. Pound in his *Cantos* turns away from his Age's 'grimace' and searches through the past (through scenes from Homer, Virgil and Chinese history) to renew contact with what is nourishing, the mysteries of Eleusis for example. Eliot in 'The Waste Land' turns away from the 'stony rubbish' of contemporary secular culture and finds fragments from Indian and early European thought with which to 'shore up' (as with beams) his 'ruin'. And Yeats sees 'things fall apart, the centre cannot hold' and finds his values in images of metaphysical Byzantium. My own foray into the past took place in Roman Italy and Pre-Socratic Greece, and in Japan where in my youth I discovered the practice of enlightenment in Zen meditation, and saw the unitive Zen view of the Universe in the imagery of the Ryoanji stone garden in Kyoto, as can be read in my poem, 'The Silence'. These fragments took me on to the essential medieval European vision. The only way for the artist in an unhealthy culture to recover contact with his culture's roots is to go back to the past and rediscover the vitality his culture once had in its early years (perhaps via another culture) and to reflect its early vitality in images which have creative force; and in so doing he renews his own creative vitality and transforms his own contemporary culture by putting it in touch with its common ground of belief during past growth.

In philosophy, history and literature, there is salvation today in going back to the past. In philosophy, metaphysical Reality was abandoned around 1910; the vision of the metaphysical Whole was abandoned like a disused Cornish tin mine, and some philosophers need to return to 1910 and Einstein's discoveries and continue going forward from there, connecting themselves to the long mining tradition of Empirical metaphysical inquiry. Despite Toynbee, history has failed to see all differing civilizations and cultures as parts of a Whole, as one interconnecting flow (Heracleitus would have said 'flux') of events, and is not revealing the full pattern of human life but merely reductionist slices of a particular nation's history in a particular decade. Historians need to return to Toynbee's example and go forward from there, seeking patterns in the metaphysical Whole as I have tried to do in *The Fire and the*

Stones. After Pound, Eliot and Yeats (who stood firm to the end of their lives, as can be seen from Pound's later *Cantos*, Eliot's *Four Quartets* and Yeats' 'Byzantium' poems), literature failed to present a vision of the metaphysical Whole, and Kingsley Amis saying 'Nobody wants any more poems on the grander themes' in 1956 is a consequence of its academicist Augustanism or neo-Rationalism (in which statement was preferred to image). Literature has abandoned the metaphysical vision of Yeats and Eliot (who followed the occult and Christian traditions) and is heading for a secular wilderness of increasingly techniquey self-consciousness. Writers need to return to the metaphysical Whole that was still known in Tennyson's day as well as during the Modernist concern with civilization.

By in the first instance reviving the essence of European culture, such a latter-day Pre-Raphaelite Group may seem to run counter to multi-culturalism. It is fair enough that as the European nations had empires, ex-colonials should be writing in English (Rushdie about India, Walcott about the Caribbean, Soyinka about Africa), but secular treatments of the Moslem religion, however interesting in their own right, do not do much to reconnect us to the European civilization's metaphysical idea, and to that extent multi-culturalism (another term for the cultural diversity found in declining civilizations) has not helped European writers rediscover their cultural vitality and purity within the essential European vision and its common ground. On the spectrum of European literature which rightly includes multi-cultural, ex-colonial diversity, literature that revives the European civilization's essential vision must have a prominent, if not central, place. The very fact that I should have to say this is a measure of how much the metaphysical has been marginalized by the secular in our time (which is another way of saying that in our time secularized literature has lost contact with the metaphysical Search).

A European and world common culture can come from reviving the essence of European culture, the vision that began our culture's metaphysical growth, for this is at one with the essence of all other cultures. As I have shown in *The Fire and the Stones*, on the Universalist principle that all the metaphysical ideas of all 25 civilizations are the same, each essential vision has a universal aspect and is universal to all cultures. If each living civilization revives the essence of its early culture, which on the Universalist principle has the same vision behind it as every other living civilization, then internationally and globally there will be different, diverse revivals of metaphysical ideas which are essentially the same. A worldwide movement, in which each civilization returns to its metaphysical idea, would create the common ground from which every civilization could opt to join a world association that can bring an era of peace. A return to the unity of European culture could therefore mark the beginning of a Universalist movement to unite all cultures round a revival of their initial unity, and therefore of a worldwide movement for world peace. Certainly, such a worldwide movement to create a common culture based on the Fire or Light of every civilization can only be good for world peace. The contemplative practice of Universalist metaphysics is conducive to world harmony, not discord. Universalism is a metaphysical movement but it also has the potentiality to take regional blocs towards world peace.

*

I have said that the Revolution is a restoration of the metaphysical, mystical Tradition in opposition to humanism, Rationalism, Empiricism, materialism, mechanism, scepticism, positivism and reductionism. I have said that it renews the Vitalism of early 20th century philosophy (the view that life originates in a vital principle, not chemical and other physical forces) and can reunify and renew our fragmented culture round our civilization's central idea, so that Western artists and composers reflect the One. Interested practitioners – thinkers, writers, artists, composers and sculptors – need to come forward. Otley Hall will be the centre for the Revolution's ideas. Bartholomew Gosnold came to Otley Hall as a revolutionary; he sailed across the Atlantic and in 1607 founded the Jamestown settlement, which became America as we know it and which has had a huge effect on European culture. Once again, Otley Hall can have an impact on our European culture.

Like Marvell or Voltaire, I have been at peace in my Garden – in the hours I spend in the idyllic, moated, medieval and Tudor tranquillity of Otley Hall, following the contemplative life which is expressed in my poems, understanding our Age and (I am told) ahead of my time in my own philosophy, history and literature – but I cannot ignore the active life and the parlous state of our culture. I am discontented with the existing cultural order and oppose it. And so I have left my Garden (which is not unlike Marvell's Garden at Nun Appleton House, Yorkshire, or Voltaire's Garden at Château du Ferny, Switzerland, where he turned aside from the affairs of state and planted beech and chestnut) to stand on the barricades on the outermost margins of our Kingdom by the shores of the North Sea and make a Declaration. I call for support to start a necessary change so that we begin the 21st century with true values reflected somewhere on the metaphysical-secular spectrum of our culture, with signs of cultural health rather than terminal disease.

The Declaration or manifesto summarizes what the Universalist Revolution believes, in 12 points. The Universalist Revolution declares:

1   The phenomenal world of the senses is not ultimate reality. There is an invisible infinite world behind the finite one. This perception challenges and sweeps aside humanism, materialism, Rationalism, Empiricism, scepticism, mechanism, positivism and reductionism in all disciplines.

2   We can know the One beyond and behind the phenomenal world of the senses, the vision of the metaphysical Reality of Fire or Light.

3   Each one of us is therefore not a reductionist collection of atoms on a dunghill whose mind is mere brain function, or a solely social ego, but a being with an immortal, invisible body within his or her visible body (as the long mystical Tradition holds), a soul and spirit with consciousness of the infinite.

4   Universalism, a post-Existentialist development of Vitalism, states the Universe in terms of metaphysical Being, or Fire or Light, which manifests into the structure of the Universe. It is a science that studies the structure of the universal Whole, which includes every possible concept of the mind and the metaphysical layers of manifesting Being. It also studies perception of the One, the soul's experience of the Fire or Light, which is received in consciousness and can be reported phenomenologically (through a study of consciousness

or perception) in 'self-reports' which are quasi-empirical.

It is also a practical contemplative philosophy that 'existentializes' metaphysical Reality, whose universal energy can be known existentially in the contemplative vision. It contacts the universal energy of the Fire or Light, the metaphysical Reality, and applies its consequences to all disciplines. Universalism focuses on all human beings in the world and does not confine its attention to Christians or any one group.

5   The central idea of our European civilization and culture, and of all civilizations and cultures, is the metaphysical vision of Reality as Fire or Light which is beyond the world of the senses but knowable within the universal Whole.

6   This documented vision of Reality should be reinstated in philosophy to sweep away logical positivism, linguistic analysis, structuralism and Existentialism.

7   This vision of Reality has inspired the growth of all civilizations in history. History studies the universal Whole and should have a global perspective, and the metaphysical vision which is common to all civilizations is the best basis for a common world culture.

8   This vision of Reality should have a place in the spectrum of literature – novels, plays and poems – and exist alongside and challenge secular, technique-oriented literature which has nothing to say. Literature misleads if it conveys an exclusively surface view of life, if it assumes that appearances are all and does not hint at Reality. Literature should be Truth-bearing and glimpse or reveal metaphysical Reality or Being.

Universalist literature is neo-Baroque as it combines the metaphysical and secular and unites the world of the senses and spirit by seeking the sunburst experience and unity. It reveals harmony between apparent opposites: sacred and profane, regular and irregular, order and disorder, stillness and movement, Becoming and Being, time and eternity. Universalist literature combines Classicism and Romanticism, statement and image, social situations and sublime metaphysical vision, traditional and organic form.

9   Universalist philosophy, history and literature offer a vision of harmony, meaning and order in relation to

the universal Whole after the angst and anxiety of
20th-century thought (Existentialist philosophy and
Modernist literature). Universalism emphasizes the
contemplative gaze, union with the universal Whole and
the rustic pursuit of reflection amid tranquillity, the
vision of mystic writers, artists and sculptors.

10 European artists – practitioners in painting, music,
architecture and sculpture as well as literature – should
transmit the sap of the cross-disciplinary vision of the One
Fire or Light in their works and connect themselves to the
Universalist Revolution's revitalization of the European
civilization's central idea. They will thereby contribute
to the return of a common, unified European culture.

11 European culture needs to be re-formed to restore (to use
Arnold's words) the most perfect works from the best
self, which constitute the highest expressions of culture,
and to reconnect philosophy, history and literature to the
Tradition of the unity of vision of the metaphysical Fire
or Light. The Revolution should have a hearing, which
will spread awareness of the consequences for European
culture of the Revolution's fundamental shift in perception.

12 On the Universalist principle that all the metaphysical
ideas of all the 25 civilizations are essentially the same
vision, a revival of the common metaphysical vision in
the European civilization and culture will be essentially
the same as corresponding revivals in all civilizations
and cultures. The revival within the European culture
can therefore inspire an international Universalist
movement to focus on the common metaphysical ground
of all cultures and create a world culture, which would
be a force for world peace in the 21st century.

The implementation of this Declaration will have the following
consequences in modern European thought and culture:

1 Renewal within our secularized, humanistic culture, which
is in terminal decay.

2 Restoration of a vision reflected in all the European arts
over hundreds of years, round which all civilizations
have grown and whose renewal revives our culture and

revitalizes our civilization.

3   Identification of the unifying principle in the Universe of physics and formulation of a full Grand Unifying Theory (Form from Movement Theory).

4   Renewal of philosophy through a new metaphysical philosophy of the 1990s, Universalism, which challenges logical positivism, linguistic analysis and Existentialism.

5   Introduction of a new global perspective in history through a new history which takes account of all civilizations and cultures, not just slices of nation-state history, and identifies the unifying principle in all civilizations.

6   Restoration of the essential European vision in literature through a new literature which mixes the metaphysical and secular as did Baroque art (thus neo-Baroque literature), which draws on many disciplines and reflects our Age.

7   Revival of culture by a Group of practitioners who revive the essential European vision in their work, acting like a Pre-Raphaelite Group.

My Declaration exists both at the level of contemplation and at the level of action. It is a programme for change which demands reflection and requires action. A lot of work, in the form of papers and essays, needs to be done to achieve this programme. A lot of books need to be written about the Revolution's fundamental shift in perception. Philosophers, historians and writers must come forward to co-create the work of the Revolution.

The Declaration is rooted in a Tradition that is vital and energy-giving. All practitioners who submerge their identities in the Tradition and die away from abiding and functioning alone will 'bring forth much fruit' in their works. All who are interested in the vision and feel that our higher culture has been under-achieving in relation to its metaphysical potential, and agree with the Declaration should stand up and be counted.

There is a need for a fundamental change in attitude in the mainstream media, a sudden and abrupt change, not a gradual one over twenty years, because we simply can't wait any longer. And nor can the younger generation who have for too long been fed a rotten secular diet in their courses at schools and universities.

The time is now right for this long-overdue and much-needed

movement for restoration of what is 'best' in our culture. Whitehead wrote in his *Introduction to Mathematics* (1911), 'Operations of thought are like cavalry charges in a battle – they are strictly limited in number, they require fresh horses, and must only be made at decisive moments.' The world-view of humanism is coming to an end. We are entering a new stage in the pattern of our civilization. The decisive moment has arrived to bring about a fundamental change in thought before the dawn of the new century.

IN THE GARDEN OF THE ONE

Having been in Japan for four years in the 1960s as an Invited Foreign Professor at universities in Tokyo, I learned how oblique and lateral Zen thinking can be. Seekers who go to a Zen temple and say they are seeking the One are given a hoe or a broom and told to hoe or sweep the garden. There is no rational explanation: Seekers have to work out that they are supposed to be clearing and sweeping clean their own soul (which is like an overgrown garden). Seekers are told to sit and count their breaths without being told they are supposed to be looking for reality, satori, enlightenment. In considering the One in relation to gardens and how it has come through in my writings, I too shall have to be somewhat oblique, in the Zen way.

One of the turning-points of my life was a visit I made to a Zen garden in Kyoto while I was in Japan. It was in December 1965, while I was writing my long narrative poem 'The Silence' (which is about a young man's search for Truth through the conflicting multiplicity and opinions of the world of Seeming and the illusions of the many, and his awakening to mysticism and the One). In those days I went once a week to the Bank of Japan and gave the Vice-Governor a tutorial – I remember Lord Cromer, Governor of the Bank of England, phoning during one lesson and asking if Japan would bail out Harold Wilson's Labour economy and I nodded encouragingly and helped the decision forward – and as a thank-you I was taken to Kyoto and shown the temples by a Bank of Japan official. He took me to the Zen Ryoanji Garden where I saw a lot of pebbles and a few rocks. Every day a monk rakes the pebbles a different way, sometimes in swirls. The Bank of Japan official, my escort, said it was very difficult to understand the meaning of the garden, and that many Japanese ponder on the rational explanation of this garden. But intuitively I immediately saw what the garden was trying to say: all existence is of one material (atom-like pebbles or stones) and the rocks can look like rocks in sea, mountains in clouds or hills on earth. Or as I put it in 'The Silence' (1965-6):

> 'And in that four-sided garden
> rock and sea and sand
> mountain and cloud and earth
> mirrored in an empty mind
> reveal a refutable truth
> between stone and stone
> in an arbitrary frame
> there is no difference, all is one
> still or moving, all existence is the same ....'

The Zen experience of Oneness is intuitive, not rational. It is seen and experienced; not thought. But later when the leading Japanese authority on Zen (my phonetic namesake, Haga) asked me to explain my perception and I reported what my intuition told me, he said, 'You have understood. That is the meaning of the stone garden.' (One of Eliot's most fundamental experiences involved a garden: the stone pool in the rose-garden in 'Burnt Norton'.)

The vision of the One is found in the earliest civilizations, including the Old European, Mesopotamian and Egyptian civilizations. In Western philosophy, it goes back to the Pre-Socratic Greeks for whom poetry and philosophy were inseparable, and who wrote their philosophy in poems. Parmenides of Elea (who flourished c500 or possibly 450 BC) composed a poem in two books of hexameters which he called *The Way of Truth* and *The Way of Seeming*. A Greek living in Italy, he was in revolt against Pythagoras's tradition of Greek religious philosophy. He rejected the observations of the Pythagoreans, the way of the senses (Seeming), and in 'Fragment 8' approached reality, the 'One, continuous' (Truth) which was uncreated and eternal. For him all change was an illusion of sense. His contemporary Heracleitus of Ephesus, who also flourished c500 BC, put it the other way round but also approached the One: *panta rhei*, everything is in flux, everything actually changes, but behind it all is the 'ever-living' Fire ('Fragment 30'), the One. Plato listened to Parmenides and took from him the idea that the world of the senses is an illusion. Plato also listened to Heracleitus, and took from him the idea of the Fire that throws shadows (the world of the senses) on the wall of the cave.

Goethe, the first Romantic poet, author of the verse play *Faust*, parts 1 and 2 and a scientist who had an original theory of colour, was also fascinated by the One and the wholeness of Nature, and his approach was organic and the opposite of Descartes'. Descartes started with multiplicity and reduced it to unity. Descartes incorporated atomism from Greek philosophy – from Anaxagoras of Clazomenae and from Democritus (both 5th century BC) – as did Galileo, and Descartes says that what we experience of the world is an illusion; reality is what can be handled by mathematical methods. He derives the underlying mathematical idea of unity from multiplicity – he looks at different triangles and sees what they have in common, he looks for unity in multiplicity, rationally and reductionistically, and for him statements of mathematical relationships between phenomena suggest the unifying laws of Nature. Goethe's thinking, on the other hand, is organic, not mathematical. He starts with a pre-existing unity and derives multiplicity from it intuitively, and so a plant is one organ and all the different organs in a plant (leaf, petal, sepal, stamen) are one organ. He starts with Oneness and looks for multiplicity in unity, how different plants come from the One. Goethe is groping towards this idea in his didactic, Lucretius-like poem 'The Metamorphosis of Plants' (1798). It begins:

> 'You are confused, belovèd, by the thousandfold mingled multitude of flowers all over the garden. You listen to their many names which are for ever, one after another, ringing outlandishly in your ears. All their shapes are similar, yet none is the same as the next; and thus the whole chorus of them suggests a secret law, a sacred riddle.'

As much as the Zen philosopher, Goethe understands that the Universe is One, a dynamic Whole – the Wholeness of Nature – which pervades its parts. The Romantic Wordsworth (who with Coleridge brought out the *Lyrical Ballads* in 1798 after they visited Germany in 1797) saw this in Book 1 of *The Prelude* (which he began in 1798) when he refers to the 'Wisdom and Spirit of the Universe' that has 'unknown modes of being'. In 'Tintern Abbey'

(1798) this spirit 'rolls through all things'. His friend Coleridge saw the Wholeness of Nature when he wrote of the 'esemplastic power of the imagination' – 'esemplastic' meaning 'shaping into One'. Shelley wrote in 'Adonais' (which is about the death of Keats):

> 'The One remains, the many change and pass;...
> Life, like a dome of many-coloured glass
> Stains the white radiance of Eternity.'

The Romantic (Goethe, Wordsworth, Coleridge, Shelley) looked at a garden and shaped it with his imagination, saw its many flowers as an expression of the One, a dynamic Whole whose operation and process is the main law of Nature.

My own work is in this Pre-Socratic and Romantic tradition. My Collected Poems mix philosophy and poetry as do the Pre-Socratics and are called *A White Radiance*, echoing that quotation from Shelley. I emphasize the metaphysical aspect – how Nature came from the One which is beyond Nature – more than the Romantics did, and look back to Metaphysical poetry, for example, Marvell's 'Garden' (the crowning glory of our contemplative verse). When Marvell was about 30, he became tutor to Mary, the daughter of General Fairfax, the victor of Naseby who had disagreed with Cromwell's policy and retired to his estate at the Fairfax home, Nun Appleton House, Yorkshire. Marvell was there from 1651 to 1652 and he wrote of the Garden there as a paradise in which there was contact with metaphysical Light:

> 'Here at the Fountains sliding foot,
> Or at some Fruit-trees mossy root,
> Casting the Bodies Vest aside,
> My Soul into the boughs does glide:
> There like a Bird it sits, and sings,
> Then whets, and combs its silver Wings;
> And, till prepar'd for longer flight,
> Waves in its Plumes the various Light.'

I visited Marvell's Garden in October 1973 and wrote 'A Metaphysical in Marvell's Garden', rooting myself in Marvell's contemplative tradition. Using the imagery of the Garden as it is today, I describe the dynamic One that pours its energy into

Nature, as the first five stanzas illustrate:
    'The House is hidden down lanes of the mind,
    It stands "Strictly Private" amid green fields,
    Over the redbrick front, a weathercock.
    Behind, sunny lawns. Shaped evergreen shields
    A huge cedar. And here a long green pond
    Winds past the stone arch of a nun's chapel.
    A Roman tomb ponders the October,
    Among the ragged roses remember Marvell.

    Here shed the body like a sheepskin jacket,
    Discard all thought as in a mystery school.
    By this nun's grave sit and be the moment,
    A oneness gazing on the heart's green pool.
    A Universe unfolds between two stone columns
    And takes a leafy shape on clouded ground.
    The sun-lily floats. Question its waters,
    It will trickle through your fingers and be drowned.

    The South Front sundial says in coloured glass
    "Qui Est Non Hodie". I am a bowl.
    In the North Hall the piano-tuner
    Ping ping pings and trembles through my soul.
    Who would not live in this delicious quiet,
    Walk among columns, lie on the grass and wait?
    Who would not teach a Fairfax daughter here,
    Escape all bills, be free to contemplate

    A flowered soul rooted like a climbing rose,
    A metaphysical swoon of gold moments
    Whose images curl down through thorns and leaves
    (Wit and wordplay), spirit and satin sense,
    Petalled layers and folds of whorled meaning
    In whose dew-perfumed bowls a divine breeze blows;
    Or like the prickly flame of the firethorn
    Which crackles where purgation merely glows?

    With drowsed eyes glance at solid grass and be
    In whirlpools of energy, like a sea.
    Breaths heave the light, and answering currents pour

Through spongy stones and stars, or seaweed tree.
Now see with eye of mind into swelled form,
Imagine sap wash, oak wave in acorn.
Knowers are one with known, and are soaked by tides
That foam and billow through an ebbing lawn.'

Many of my poems glimpse the One in a more lyrical mode and widen the Garden into the Universe. Sometimes the One is barely understood, as in my early poem, 'Flow: Moon and Sea' (1971):

'I loved you like the tortoise-shell
You loved up on the Downs with me.
The light leaps off your Worthing sea
Like shoals of leaping mackerel.

The sea flows like a bent hawthorn.
Now, up the night, the harvest moon
Floats and sails like a child's balloon
Over this darkly rippled corn.

This glow behind the moon and sea
Affects my way of seeing.
What, oh what is happening to my being?
I thrill to a pebble's flow, and a bumble-bee.'

In my later poems, the One *is* understood. In my poem 'The One and the Many' (1992) I encounter the One during a walk in the Cornish harbour where I have a house twenty yards from the sea wall with a view over the sweep of the bay, the harbour cliffs and Smeaton's early 1790s jetty or 'pier' which is almost part of the front garden:

'A late night walk. The moon is full
Beside the cliff with a sloping side
That joins the dark sea and curves back
Where its black shadows lap with the tide.

Transfixed on the pier, I stare, I stare
As the moon-like One manifests through space
Into the Being of a silhouette

And its reflection in existing place.
Transfixed on the pier, I gaze, I gaze,
At a moonlit void where – mystery! – lurks
A sloping Being and its shadow,
I gaze at how the Universe works.

A late night walk, and a spring in my step
As I tread the granite back to my home
And sit agog that the One has shone
Into sloping things that have stained it with foam.'

This emphasis on a metaphysical One that pours energy from beyond Nature and manifests into the Universe, which came out of nothing, is a feature of Universalism, a philosophy the Pre-Socratic Parmenides and Heracleitus would have no difficulty in understanding. They would support my Form from Movement theory in which all form came from a pre-existing moving Fire, the metaphysical Fire Eliot was referring to when he spoke of the fire and the rose being one at the end of 'Little Gidding', for it is the One of Parmenides and the 'ever-living' Fire of Heracleitus ('Fragment 30').

This Fire found its way into my philosophical poem 'The Laughing Philosopher' (1993). It is set in Ficino's Renaissance Florence, and I end the poem by reflecting on a painting by Bramante of Heracleitus and Democritus, in which the materialistic Democritus is laughing and the metaphysical Heracleitus is weeping. (A magnifying glass shows two tears trickling down each of his cheeks.) In the last stanza I say it should be the other way round:

'In a picture in Milan by Bramante
Two philosophers stand by a globe, one sad, one gay.
Democritus knew atoms before Rutherford's ball,
He laughs because men believe transience is all.
Heracleitus weeps as all believe "everything flows"
And no one sees the Fire – which he himself knows,
And so should smile. Sad Ficino, laugh and inspire:
For all is flux, but underneath – the Fire!'

This metaphysical idea of the Fire has immense consequences in history, for all civilizations rise following a vision of the Fire and decline when the vision ceases to be renewed and they turn secular. Such a view of history is Universalist for it sees all history as a Whole whose One ramifies (to use an organic word) into many civilizations. It is history done with organic thinking such as Goethe would have appreciated.

This Oneness is the central idea of many of my short stories, some of which are poetic revelations of Being, and of my poetic epic *Overlord*, which is in 12 books like the *Aeneid* and *Paradise Lost*. *Overlord* is a latter-day *Iliad* about the struggle between Eisenhower and Hitler, with Christ and Satan (and angels and devils) also struggling in Heaven and Hell. One cannot write about cosmic struggles in Heaven mirroring those on earth without stating clearly how the Universe came into being, and early in Book 1 there is an account of how everything – the many – came from the One. In the opening pages I write of the unity – oneness – of the 12 books in terms of a plant, Jack-by-the-hedge, which has 12 leaves:

> '...as I gaze at a hedge I see
> I grow a white vision like a wild plant –
> Please come to my aid with heroic verse
> In twelve books like twelve leaves on the stem of
> Jack-by-the-hedge (garlic mustard) which grows
> Wild in hedgerows and ends in a white flower.'

The One is behind all Nature and all disciplines – history, physics, metaphysical philosophy, literature – and I hold that the vision of the One has inspired the profoundest insights of the great philosophers and poets (Plato, Dante, Milton), and the growth of the European civilizations. I maintain that today we have more or less lost this vision – we are lost in multiplicity – and we need to get back to the vision of the One. My Revolution in Modern Thought and Culture restores the traditional vision of European civilization's unified culture as opposed to its present culture which is split apart in secular diversity. The metaphysical vision of the Fire and divine Light – the saint with the halo – once united European civilization, its sap permeated the trunk of the Christian religion and the diverse branches of its culture, its philosophy, history and literature and all the other disciplines. My call for a revitalization of the sap of European culture seeks to reconnect European culture to the Garden of the One so it rediscovers itself as a garden of the One.

The garden at Otley Hall – a Tudor moated hall in Suffolk, England dating back to 1190, which was rebuilt c1450-1525 and which the public come to see – has ten acres of grounds, and I have had the idea of re-creating some pre-Tudor and Tudor features. I have asked Sylvia Landsberg, author of *The Medieval Garden* (a British Museum book) and designer of five of the six historically accurate re-created English Tudor gardens open to the public, to design a historically accurate herber, a knot and herb garden and other Tudor features. The knot garden has 25 beds, one for each civilization of *The Fire and the Stones*, and the cer ...i knot suggests the metaphysical One that is central to the many just as surely as does the stone garden in Kyoto, Japan. We have planned three knots in different places – Princess Elizabeth's knot (1544), The Gardener's Labyrinth (1577) and the fleur de luce (1580-1617), whose fleur-de-lis or lily is all over the 1330 and 1450 parts of Otley Hall's Great Hall and Linenfold Room. (The fleur-de-lis was originally called 'fleur de Louis' after the French king Louis VII. It was the yellow lily that was the emblem on his shield when he went on the Second Crusade in the 12th century. He arrived in Jerusalem in 1148. It was sacred to Mary, and was adopted from the French royal arms into the British royal arms by Edward III in 1337 and redesigned by Henry V in 1400. Thus in England it represents France, part of which was under British rule for much of the 14th century.) At another level the knot also represents the soul, and I am reminded of a little book called *The Lily of Light* which sees the soul in terms of agricultural stages, an idea I worked out in my long poem, 'The Weed-Garden', which portrays the Garden that is modern England and the modern English soul as overgrown and in need of clearing.

At Otley Hall we can relive the beginnings of our modern Western (European and American) history. The lily motif recalls the time when England and France were united from Edward III to Henry V. The linenfold panelling is linked with Cardinal Wolsey, and the US was arguably founded from Otley Hall in as much as Bartholomew Gosnold's two famous voyages were planned round its hearth. His 1602 voyage, funded by the Earl of Southampton, Shakespeare's patron, named Martha's Vineyard, and his 1606/7 voyage founded the Jamestown settlement 13 years before the *Mayflower* set sail. In more recent times, Otley Hall was linked with Sir Oswald Mosley and was intended to be Hitler's southern HQ in Britain had he won a seaborne Battle of Britain – a shadow I hope I have banished with my two-part verse play *The Warlords* (which is about Montgomery) and my poetic epic *Overlord*. As much as Voltaire's Garden it will be a Garden where the philosophically-minded can reflect on history, philosophy, metaphysics and literature. The sundial has a motto: 'Amyddst ye fflowres I tell ye houres.' 'Houres' must be understood in its historical sense of 'centuries' as well as in its philosophical sense of 'passing moments'.

The Otley Hall gardens are open to the public on certain days as is the house, and our progress can be observed as we re-create a Garden of the One whose Tudor herbs and flowers convey the idea of the One as clearly as do the pebbles and rocks of the Japanese stone garden.

NOTES

1 Dr W A Visser't Hooft, *No Other Name: The Choice between Syncretism and Christian Universalism,* Westminster Press, Philadelphia, Pennsylvania, USA, 1963.
2 Arnold Toynbee, *A Study of History,* vol 7, OUP, UK, 1954, p428 n2.
3 Quoted by R Runcie in *World Faiths Insight,* October 1986, New Series 14, p14.
4 See for example Larry Abraham, *Call it Conspiracy*; Robert Eringer, *The Global Manipulators*; Anthony Sutton, *An Introduction to the Order* and *The Secret Cult of the Order*; James Perloff, *The Shadows of Power*; and Stan Deyo, *The Cosmic Conspiracy.*
5 Another such event was the change in the composition of the British House of Lords. British Prime Minister Blair resolved to abolish the hereditary peers' voting rights so that he could secure House of Lords' approval for constitutional changes that will break up the United Kingdom and allow a separated Scotland, Wales, Ireland, London and the 8 other Euro-regions of England to pass into a United States of Europe. This is Bilderberg policy, and it is interesting that Lord Carrington, Chairman of the Bilderberg Group, was present at the Lords during the meeting on 2 December 1998 when the Conservative Opposition leader William Hague dismissed Viscount Cranborne, Conservative leader in the House of Lords (both of whom have attended Bilderberg meetings). Cranborne, a descendant of the Elizabethan Cecils, had met Blair without Hague's knowledge and agreed a deal that would preserve the voting rights of 91 hereditary peers in return for allowing free passage to government constitutional legislation in the Lords.
6 On 28 February 1994 for the first time ever NATO planes were used in an offensive, combat role rather than in self-defence, and were directed to shoot down four Serbian planes on UN orders, making NATO a branch of a world army under UN control and therefore under the control of the Committee of 300.
7 See John Cotter, *A Study in Syncretism (The Background and Apparatus of the Emerging One World Church),* Canadian Intelligence Publications, 1979, p103.
8 My declaration of the Revolution was made in the Jubilee Hall, Aldeburgh, Suffolk. The hall is by the North Sea, and it was possible to regard the Revolution as taking the form of a march on London.

APPENDIX 1

TWO INTERVIEWS WITH NICHOLAS HAGGER
ON THE PUBLICATION OF
THE UNIVERSE AND THE LIGHT 1993

These two interviews were conducted on behalf of Midas, but were never used. They are included for the light they throw on the origins and early formation of Universalism and for phrases such as 'process metaphysics'.

Q What is the book doing?

A It presents the Universe in terms of the Light, the hidden reality and energy behind the Universe and Nature which pre-existed the Big Bang and flows into the soul and is known in all religions. It therefore offers a new view of man and the Universe in which man is like a sponge in a sea of Light. It integrates all disciplines including history in terms of a hidden reality, and presents a Theory of Everything that includes love and conversation and not just materialistic forces. It presents a new philosophy of Universalism (a philosophy of the Light). It opposes materialism in the sciences and philosophy and advances a metaphysical science (Bergson's 'much desired union of science and metaphysics'). It effects a Metaphysical Revolution. It reunifies the Universe and knowledge. It changes people's way of looking and their perspective in relation to the books on school and university syllabuses, and seeks to effect a revolution in thought. It makes metaphysics respectable again after 90 years, and coincides with Iris Murdoch's *Metaphysics as a Guide to Morals*. It carries forward the tradition of Donne, Coleridge, Graves and Eliot. Eliot's *Four Quartets* includes snippets from all disciplines, but everything has moved on since the 1940s and this book updates the Tradition and takes account of the advances of the last fifty years.

Q What is the book saying?

A 'The Nature of Light' shows that the Light is known to all mystics in all cultures and civilizations as was established in *The Fire and the Stones*, and is widely considered to be God. The vision of the Light is the central idea of all civilizations, which grow when it is strong and passes into their religions, and decline when it weakens, leaving their religions hollow. The Light is behind Nature, cosmology and consciousness. It manifests from the One into latent Non-Being (the quantum vacuum) and into Being and thence into Existence, pouring particles into Nature and creating both matter and consciousness (which is an electromagnetic spectrum). The immaterial Light provides cosmology with the Grand Unified Theory it has failed to reach at the materialistic level alone, and unites all four forces within its own fifth force (expanding, manifesting Light which Newton sought) and presses particles into apparently random, but in fact organized, uncertainty.

The Light makes possible a Metaphysical Revival or Restoration, as it reunites ontology (the study of the hidden Reality behind Nature, the Light) with spiritual psychology (the location of our deeper self which receives the Reality 'across the bridge' from the rational, social ego), epistemology (how this Reality is known through meditation) and cosmology (the structure of the physical Universe which can only be understood in relation to the Reality). Such a view extends Romanticism.

'What is Universalism?' defines Universalism as showing the universal energy of the Fire or Light pouring into the universal being (soul/spirit) from the Universe with great universality. All humankind regardless of civilization or religion has the experience, which is therefore common to all religions. The Light is seen through the 'eye of contemplation' (Bonaventure), not the eye of reason or the bodily eye, and it makes possible a new view of man – man open to energy and forces in the Universe – and a new view of the Universe as non-materialistic energy in which all particles are charged with the Light. The Light is Newton's expanding force, Einstein's cosmological constant and Bohm's hidden variability, and it gives all particles their mass. It is possible that its effects will be deduced by the best ever particle smasher, the Large Hadron Collider.

In offering this new view of man, Universalism solves problems the Romantics and Modernists left unsolved, for Universalism approaches reality on a regular basis through meditation. The changed view of man and the Universe must lead to changes in science and philosophy, as the changed view signals the end for reductionism (that there is nothing non-material) and logical positivism (that the logic of the rational, social ego can explain away all non-material energy and abolish all invisible metaphysical reality). There needs to be a revolution in science and philosophy to change the way they are taught in universities. The revolution also involves a practical change in one's own life through meditation and contemplation of the Light when one is ready.

'Reductionism, Holism and Universalism' shows that reductionism (the view that biological and mental events can be reduced to physical events) is materialistic and physicalist, and so is holism, which sees the Whole as immeasurable and perhaps infinite, but as spatial and non-transcendental. The same is true of all theories regarding self-organizing and complexity. The metaphysical alternative to reductionism is not holism but Universalism, which presents the All at all levels and makes possible a metaphysical science, a true view. Such a change picks up the thread of philosophy in 1910 (William James, Bergson, T E Hulme, Whitehead and Husserl) and science c1917 (Einstein and Whitehead).

Appendix 1 summarizes a Grand Unified Theory of history and shows how the rise of civilizations happens through the central idea of Fire or Light and a god, how a new people introduce a heretical god, and how civilizations fall through federalism and foreign occupation. It shows how the major religions share key themes and the most important religious events in civilizations.

Appendix 2 explains how the creation of the Universe began as a movement of the Fire or Light before the Big Bang or hot beginning, and there are some mathematical symbols.With the possible exception of Heracleitus, this is the first time an origin of the Universe has been proposed in terms of a movement rather than a stillness, and this is an original creation theory in its own right.

Appendix 3 shows how evolution has been a process of manifestation from the Light rather than a neo-Darwinian or neurophysiological materialistic phenomenon. This is a Universalist view of evolution.

Q **What is the Metaphysical Revolution?**

A It is a counter-revolution against 150 years of dehumanizing reductionism in physics, biology and the other sciences and 90 years of logical positivism/linguistic analysis in philosophy. It spreads metaphysical science (*see* 10 points on pp111-2) and a theory of absolutely everything including metaphysical reality, philosophical vitalism and the process metaphysics of the Fire or Light (or Universalism): philosophy as a system of general ideas that includes all possible concepts, including rather than excluding metaphysical ones. It offers a changed view of man and the Universe and therefore maintains that science's and philosophy's view of man and the Universe must change.

Metaphysics traditionally focuses on Being and Knowing. It holds that reality is supersensible, beyond the five senses (the American meaning). It is also a branch of philosophy that is the science of a universal Whole or All which includes ontology, spiritual psychology, epistemology and cosmology, all within an intuitively experienceable and rationally consistent Whole which includes all possible ideas, i.e. a system of general ideas that includes every possible concept of the mind.

Q Can you explain the idea of the Light?

A It is a spiritual sun or white light which mystics of all times have seen. It is dazzlingly bright, seen behind closed eyes. According to the Tradition, it is of divine origin and comes into the soul from the beyond. It is the Quaker Inner Light, the Christian Divine Light (of Christ, the Light of the World), the Orthodox Transfiguration, Islamic Sufi fana, Hindu samadhi, Tantric Hinduism's kundalini, Mahayana Buddhist enlightenment, the Tibetan Buddhist Clear Light of the Void, the Taoist Formless or Subtle Light (the Golden Flower), the Zen Buddhist satori. It is God according to the Christian tradition of St Augustine, St Gregory and St Bernard, while God is the darkness within or behind the Light according to an Eastern tradition of Dionysius the Areopagite. Hundreds of instances over the last 5,000 years are documented in Part 1 of *The Fire and the Stones*.

The Light is only known in the soul, with the eye of contemplation, at the appropriate stage on the Mystic Way when the seeker has moved back from the social ego to the soul. The main stages of the Mystic Way are: awakening from the ego, purgation (or purification, detachment from the senses, involving a shift from the 'I' of the rational, social ego to the soul/spirit), illumination (or the Illuminative Way, i.e. the soul's experience of the Light), the dark night of the soul (further spiritual cleansing and detachment of the spirit from the senses) and the unitive vision (when the Universe is perceived to be a unity). The experience of the Light rarely happens before the age of 24, and many never discover the Mystic Way. One of the purposes of the Metaphysical Revolution is to point out to the younger generation that illumination is there and that a search for it can be successful.

Q **How are you to be described?**

A I am a poet and cultural historian, philosopher and man of letters. I am a pupil of the Empsonian literary critic Christopher Ricks and taught at the same university as William Empson in Tokyo. (I was the first Invited Foreign Professor since Empson to teach at Empson's old university, Tokyo University of Education, in Japan.) In my interlocking poems, cultural history and philosophy of science (and in my diaries), I seek to reflect the Age and reveal the reality behind Nature, history and the Universe. In doing this I follow the many-sided example of Coleridge (who wrote poems and the *Biographia Literaria*, journals which united physics and German metaphysics), Robert Graves (who wrote poems, *The White Goddess*, which crosses many cultures, *The Greek Myths* and *I Claudius*) and T S Eliot (whose *Four Quartets* were cross-disciplinary, and who wrote *Notes towards the Definition of Culture* and *Idea of a Christian Society*). T S Eliot's shoes have never been filled. I visited Ezra Pound in Italy in 1970, and Eliot's friend E W F Tomlin (author of *T S Eliot, A Friendship* and metaphysical philosopher of *The Approach to Metaphysics* and *Philosophers of East and West*) was my boss in Japan (as Representative of the British Council).

Very few literary figures have researched at a high level into many disciplines. Lawrence Durrell was influenced by Einstein's four-dimensional space-time in his *Alexandrian Quartet*, but C P Snow in *Two Cultures* complained that generally writers are illiterate in matters of science.

I have been at pains to go to the heart of our civilization and culture. If it is true that the Light is the central idea of civilizations as *The Fire and the Stones* claims, then the poet, cultural historian and philosopher who reflects the Light is renewing the central idea of our civilization and is producing work of fundamental importance.

*

Q Three scientists and two philosophers have endorsed *The Universe and the Light*, which covers many developments in science and philosophy, but your previous books were in the fields of poetry and history. You are very wide-ranging?

A Or cross-disciplinary. My background is in English Literature. Having studied under Christopher Ricks, who writes in the tradition of William Empson (a devotee of Donne), I became a Professor of English Literature and a practising poet in Japan in the 1960s at Empson's old university. Out there I was told Empson got the sack in 1934 after returning nude in a taxi after bathing, a fate I managed to avoid. The philosopher E W F Tomlin, a friend of T S Eliot's, was living in Tokyo and I had many conversations with him and contributed to a book of memorial essays to mark Eliot's death, which Tomlin edited. I widened into philosophy and history in Tokyo. I was asked to teach a course to the PhD students on Gibbon, Spengler and Toynbee and saw a fourth way of accounting for the rise and fall of civilizations. It took me twenty-five years to do the research and put it down on paper, but that became *The Fire and the Stones*. Like Donne, Marvell, Milton, Coleridge and Graves, Eliot combined poetry with an interest in philosophy and culture, which informs both his poems and his essays. As yet no one has taken Eliot's place. I am consciously carrying forward Eliot's tradition in a different, non-Christian way, by looking at the Universe as a Whole, seeing Nature, civilizations, cultures, religion, science and philosophy as integrated aspects of a Whole. There are many specialists, but too few who are wide-ranging. I never met Eliot but I visited Eliot's friend Ezra Pound in Rapallo in 1970 and he asked me 'Can you sum up the culture of the last thirty years?' Pound was very interested in contemporary culture. *The Fire and the Stones* provides the cultural context for our European civilization's decline. *The Universe and the Light* shows where science and philosophy have gone wrong in relation to our civilization's central idea.

Q You say the central idea of our civilization is a vision of the Light?

A Yes, the Fire or Light which the mystics have known as illumination. It is to be found in 25 civilizations as I showed, and is known by mystics in all cultures at all times. *The Fire and the Stones* contains many 'eye-witness' accounts, such as Pascal's. I first glimpsed the Light in a Zen Buddhist temple while I was in Japan. The Light is widely regarded as being a vision of God. It is seen within but of course it is outside as well, for it's all One. It's as though we're sponges in a sea of Light, and the Light is both within us and all round us. In *The Fire and the Stones* I show that civilizations begin with a vision of the Fire or Light, which passes into their religions. They grow while the vision is strong and decline when it weakens. So, for example, Mohammed has a vision of the Fire in a cave, it becomes the *Koran*, Islam then grows round it as does the Arab Empire, and the civilization remains strong so long as the metaphysical vision which began it is strong. In the European civilization the vision of the Fire or Light could be found in abundance in the 17th century, in the Metaphysical poets for example, and there are still glimpses in the poets of the 19th century. In the 20th century it has almost died out. There is Yeats's 'sages standing in God's holy fire' and Eliot's 'the fire and the rose are one', but there's very little reference to it. If it is correct that the Light is our civilization's central idea, then the writer who reflects it is renewing his civilization, literally keeping it alive, preserving its identity.

Q **You have presumably often seen the mystic Light?**

A Yes. I came across the Light when studying the Metaphysical poets, and I experienced it first in Japan in 1965 and then after my return to London in 1971, when I had two very intense dramatic months of illumination from September to November. These feature in my poems and also in my diaries. You have to be a certain age to have the experience. No one really has it before 24. I had my first glimpse at 26. It's seen in the soul, and the seeker has to move back from the rational, social ego to the soul or spirit. It's like crossing a bridge over the Thames. It doesn't happen when you're in your teens and are egocentric, the centre shift (the subject of my poem 'The Silence') only happens after you've begun on the Mystic Way – after awakening and purgation – during the Illuminative Life.

Q **Has this experience been given public currency in our culture?**

A No, and more's the pity. Our 20th century European culture is ruled by the rational, social ego, which in philosophy has declared that the soul and anything 'unphenomenal' does not exist, as did the logical positivists and linguistic analysts at the beginning of the 20th century. They denied the soul and spirit and put a road-block called the verification principle across the traditional Mystic Way of St John of the Cross and Dante, and in so doing marginalized the central idea of our culture and civilization and accelerated their decline. Science has always been materialistic, sceptical, humanistic and Rationalistic and has traditionally denied that intuitive gnosis is admissible as scientific evidence. All that's changing. There's a feeling now abroad that materialistic reductionist science is no longer appropriate in our post-quantum time, and that philosophy went wrong c1910. There's a feeling that science should allow many reports of the same inner experience to be considered as evidence, and that the fundamental idea of our culture and civilization should be given currency again, as it was in the 17th century, when you could hear it preached every Sunday in every pulpit in the land.

Q **Your Metaphysical Revolution puts things right?**

A It's giving vent to a feeling that as there is a new view of humankind and the Universe – humans being open to tides of Light which flow into their soul and fill them with wisdom – then philosophy and science should change; there should be a more metaphysical view of both. In its American sense metaphysics means interest in the 'supersensible, whatever is beyond the five senses' and so the paranormal is thought of as metaphysics. But in its more primary sense, metaphysics has traditionally always been the science of the All, of a universal Whole, that focuses on Being and Knowing and includes ontology, transpersonal psychology, epistemology and cosmology in terms of the divine reality of the Light. Donne, the first Metaphysical poet, would have recognized that description of metaphysics. He called the Light the divine 'Sunne' in his *Sermons*. He criticized the new sceptical philosophy of his day in 'The First Anniversary' (1611):

'And new Philosophy calls all in doubt,
    The Element of fire is quite put out.'

Marvell would also have recognized it. One of my more central poems is called 'A Metaphysical in Marvell's Garden'. There is a feeling that it is time to restore metaphysics, which was wrongly debunked by the logical positivists who focused on the rational, social ego and its logical and analytical powers, and ignored the intuitive part of human beings that Bergson,

154

William James, T E Hulme, Whitehead and Husserl were all interested in c1910.

Q **Why 'Revolution'?**

A If you say 'There must be a gradual change', that's wishy-washy and nothing happens. The only way to move the situation forward and solve the problems is to have a sudden and abrupt change, to announce 'It's changed'. I was teaching at the University of Libya at the time of the Libyan Revolution – Gaddafi's Revolution – in September 1969. I went to work on the morning of September 1, found the gates closed, heard shooting and had to beetle home in my car through the revolution. To my knowledge no one was killed; it was a relatively bloodless coup. I'm not the greatest admirer of Gaddafi, but the old regime could not solve the problems, and so he accelerated the pace of change. That is what I am trying to do in science and philosophy – indeed all disciplines. At schools and universities throughout the country, the young are being served up texts that deny the reality behind Nature and the Universe. Think of deconstruction and Derrida, for example, and all the social humanist poems that have marginalized the mystic Tradition in literature as well as our civilization's central idea and identity. I told a group of metaphysical philosophers in Oxford, 'I am going through a hole in the hedge and I'm going to stand on the lawn of the philosophical and scientific Establishment and risk being frogmarched off to a madhouse, and if you're with me you'll come through the hedge as well and there will then be a negotiation and we will be given space again in the scientific and philosophical house.' I am endeavouring to seek that negotiation. It may turn out that we recover possession of the house that was wrongly taken over at the beginning of the century.

Q **And if there's resistance?**

A You want me to say that we will fight a battle and have cultural firing-squads! But there is a battleground. On one side are the ideas of the materialists, reductionists and atheists who tell the young that we are living on 'a dunghill of purposeless interconnected corruption' (P W Atkins), a bleak Beckett-type humanist vision. On the other side are the metaphysical thinkers and seers who have known reality in meditation and assert that on death the soul withdraws from the mind and body and attaches itself to the spirit and goes on elsewhere, who see humankind not just in terms of the body and mind (the Renaissance humanist truncated vision) but in terms of the spirit and divine spark as well (the medieval vision they are restoring).

Q **Where does your philosophy of Universalism fit into this?**

A Universalism is the metaphysical philosophy. Universalism is about all humankind. There is political Universalism (human rights for all humankind) and religious Universalism (the belief that all humankind's souls can be saved). There are two kinds of spiritual Universalism: Christian Universalism (which is about all humankind in relation to Christ) and a more syncretistic form which focuses on the common essence of *all* religions, which is of course the Fire or Light as I demonstrated in *The Fire and the Stones*. My Universalism holds that the universal energy of the Fire or Light flows into the Universe and universal being from beyond with great universality. This is denied by reductionist materialists, and if you hold this view then you cannot be a reductionist materialist. Universalism has three planks. Firstly it focuses on the universal energy common to all religions which applies to every human being in the world. Secondly, it is Universalism that will be the philosophy of the coming United States of Europe and of the coming World Government, which I see as a global phase of the North American civilization even though it will involve the United Nations. Thirdly, philosophical Universalism has replaced Existentialism, which was based on the rational, social ego and not the soul or spirit, and is dead. My Universalism is in the tradition of Romanticism, which affirmed the soul and spirit as did the poems of Wordsworth and Coleridge and other English Romantic poets.

Q **Are there metaphysical philosophers and Universalist artists?**

A Oh yes. There's the highly original thinking of the Leibnizian Geoffrey Read in philosophy – he has a new, metaphysical view of space, time, matter and memory – and philosophers like Alison Watson are developing their own manifestational philosophy. The neo-Husserlian and neo-Heideggerian Chris McCann is developing a new philosophy of Being and Becoming, and of the One. They are all in varying degrees Rationalists rather than Intuitionists like me. In art there are a number of painters who try to show the One behind the many.

Q Is metaphysics becoming respectable again?

A After 80 or 90 years of wrongly being pushed out by certain 20th-century philosophers, yes. Iris Murdoch has written *Metaphysics as a Guide to Morals*.

Q You are trying to effect a profound change in our culture. Isn't it an impossible, Herculean task?

A The metaphysical perspective has physical, psychological, spiritual and divine levels and encompasses all of them. At the physical level the need is for practical meditations that enable people to experience the spiritual, divine Light. At the psychological level, I will continue to write interlocking books that redefine knowledge in terms of the One Reality behind Nature and history, which the poets have seen and which the philosophers and scientists are now taking account of. Word is spreading, the change will happen. The cultural media – television and the so-called quality press – will be the last to latch on.

Q You have a Grand Unified Theory. Will there be a Theory of Everything?

A A Grand Unified Theory is a partial theory. In physics, a Grand Unified Theory unifies three forces, and a Theory of Everything unifies four forces. The position is that the weak and electromagnetic forces have definitely been unified, and an attempt to integrate these with the strong force works in theory but there is no evidence that it works in practice. There is no proof that gravity can be 'quantized' like the other three forces, and that there are gravitons. In physics, a Grand Unified Theory is disputed, and there is no sign of a Theory of Everything. Hawking is seeking to unify the four physical materialistic forces, but a true Theory of Everything takes the higher metaphysical levels into account. 'Everything' includes love and conversation. I have done my Grand Unified Theory: *The Fire and the Stones* is subtitled 'A Grand Unified Theory of World History and Religion'. That was the hard part, to integrate mysticism, metaphysics, religion and world history in precise historical stages, all of which have precise dates. I am now seeking to formulate a Theory of Everything by integrating physics, biology, philosophy and other disciplines. The Theory of Everything I see is very simple: the Light is behind everything and shapes it, the Light many people have called God. It is simple enough to be expressed in a simple mathematical formula such as $E = mc^2$. Are the mathematics already there in the Universe or are they human constructs we invent? I believe they're there, and that they just have to be uncovered, like scraping away sand to reveal a ruined Roman temple.

Q **You are dealing with very difficult subject matter: quantum theory and space exploration and ontology. Will people understand you?**

A No one expects a distillation of all disciplines and current knowledge to be easy. Eliot attempted such a distillation in his later poems, and was renowned for his obscurity. It's all moved on 50 years since the early 1940s, when he was working on the *Four Quartets*, and Eliot would be horrified by how complex it has all become if he came back now. Eliot, Pound and Yeats attempted to arrive at the truth about the Universe and history, and their readers have found it rewarding to grapple with their insights, just as they have found it rewarding to grapple with Jung and Einstein. Not many contemporary poets are rewarding in that sense. You won't get many insights into the Universe by grappling with Larkin's Mr Bleaney in his bedsit. I am sure readers will find it rewarding to grapple with our current distillation.

Q **If you were to die next year and could write your epitaph, what would you like it to say?**

A. You are indirectly asking my aim. I think I would like it to say: 'All his books were pieces of a jigsaw which fitted together to show one picture – the One Truth behind the multiplicity of the Age.' I think I would like it to say: 'He did not flinch from turning away from comfort and treading the Mystic Way. He saw the Light that is central to our culture and civilization and reflected it in his poetry, history and philosophy. He tried to redefine knowledge in terms of the Light, hence the Metaphysical Revolution and Universalism.' Something like that. Oh and, 'He never lost touch with practical experience.' The poem is a wonderful medium; it keeps you immediate, close to emotions and instincts, and although the emotions and instincts become less personally attached and more universal after the shift from the rational, social ego to a new centre, they are still there. A Theory of Everything is worthless if it does not include the simplest emotions and instincts.

Q **What else are you working on?**

A A Collected Poems and volume 1 of my diaries. I've kept a daily diary since 1963, and volume 1 covers the early poems and first illumination. I am working on an autobiography which is not so much about what I've done as how I've come to think as I do, with of course accounts of my experience of the Light. Basically it's about how an ordinary bloke came to have a metaphysical vision, but it's in the tradition of Yeats's *Autobiography*. Over the years I've written over 700 very short stories, and I'm working on a four-volume Collected Stories. It's a bit like Voltaire or Sartre expressing their themes in concrete, vivid, *practical* terms. And future work will have the coming world government as its theme, and will sharpen the religious Universalism of our time. It will interlock with what I've already done, as will all my works.

Q **Why are you writing so frenetically?**

A Not frenetically, just systematically. I have no axe to grind; I don't want anyone to do anything other than reconsider their view of things. I have been on a Quest. I believe I have found the Truth or Reality, and I want to reveal and share my vision of *purpose* for the common good, for the health of individuals and for the well-being of our civilization. And I want to understand our Age in its entirety. Pretty much Donne's or Marvell's or Milton's or Coleridge's or Eliot's reasons for writing, I guess.

APPENDIX 2

A HISTORICAL NOTE ON THE ILLUMINATI AND CONTEMPORARY WORLD GOVERNMENT

As my 'third way' scenario for world government (American ecumenical Protestantism looking for common ground in all civilizations, p103) differs from the other two scenarios (world government led by the UN-Illuminati and the Pope), it is important to see how the three ways interconnect in their early history.

Over the centuries, there have been two groups of Illuminati, the original mystic group who contacted God and the heretical Satanistic group who contacted the Devil. In between were occultists who unwittingly paved the way for the diabolical version.

The original Illuminati can be traced back to 1492, when Torquemada expelled the Sefardic Jews (who preserved Babylonian rather than Palestinian rituals) from Spain. They settled in France, Holland, England, Italy and the Balkans. The upheaval had effects among Spanish families and on converted Jews, and followers of Isabel de la Cruz, a Franciscan, organized centres of Illuminists ('Alumbrados', 'enlightened ones'), mystics who made direct contact with God as Light after inner purification. The Carmelite mysticism of St Teresa and St John of the Cross was influenced by the Alumbrados in the 1560s and the 1570s, and found its way to the Spanish Habsburgs. Charles V (1500-58) was king of Spain (1516-56) and emperor of the European Habsburg lands (1519-56). He personally took the Alumbrados' influence to Germany. He transferred his functions as German emperor to his brother Ferdinand I, and his Burgundian, Spanish and Italian lands to his son Philip II. Teresa reformed the Carmelite Order to restore its austere and contemplative character in keeping with the Alumbrados, and was helped by St John of the Cross. In 1579 Philip II of Spain, who knew and admired Teresa, gave her Carmelites independent jurisdiction, which was confirmed by Pope Gregory XIII.

The Alumbrados included many converted Jews. They bypassed the sacraments and were suppressed by the Inquisition. (There were edicts against them in 1568, 1574 and 1623.) They appeared in Southern France as the Illuminés in 1623, and in 1634 were led by Pierre Guérin and they too were suppressed. The

Alumbrados spread during the 16th and 17th centuries, and in Italy they were called 'Illuminati' (the plural of 'Illuminato').

The Rosicrucians were also called Illuminati, and may have been a stepping-stone to the heretical Illuminati in the 17th century. The original Illuminati clearly influenced Rosicrucianism, which in turn must have coloured the diabolical Illuminati. Rosicrucianism may have originated in ancient Egypt; its teachings drew together occultist elements from a variety of religions. According to the earliest surviving Rosicrucian document, *Fama Fraternitatis* ('Account of the Brotherhood'), published in 1614 and telling of his journey, Christian Rosenkreuz was the founder of Rosicrucianism. He was apparently born in 1378 and visited Egypt and Damascus before returning to Germany. According to another view Paracelsus, the Swiss alchemist who died in 1541, was the real founder and was responsible for the spread of Rosicrucianism in Germany.

The link between the Alumbrados and the Spanish-Austrian Habsburgs gave rise to the heretical Illuminati. The Austrian Habsburgs ruled the Holy Roman Empire in Germany from 1440 to 1806. They acquired the Netherlands, Luxembourg and Burgundy in 1477, and ruled Spain from 1504 to 1506 and 1516 to 1700. They also ruled Naples, Sicily and Sardinia. The Austrian line (known after 1740 as the House of Habsburg-Lorraine) ruled the Habsburg possessions in Central Europe until 1918. As Holy Roman Emperor, the head of the Habsburgs had close dealings with the Pope.

During the 18th century Bavaria was ravaged by the wars of Spanish and Austrian succession, and the Catholic Habsburgs were regarded as the enemy by local Bavarians. The Habsburg Joseph II sought to expand westwards into Bavaria and, following the War of the Bavarian Succession (1778-9), Prussia restricted the Habsburg gains to Innviertel in 1779 and opposed Joseph's attempt to swap the Netherlands for Bavaria in 1784.

Within this context, the Bavarian Adam Weishaupt, Professor of canon law at the University of Ingolstadt, opposed Spain and Catholicism by setting up a rival Illuminati that did not approach God but the Devil. His Masonic sect sought to replace Christianity with a 'religion' of reason. It emphasized Republican free thought, the end of the higher religions, and the achievement of brotherhood by the violent killing of many people. His heretical, diabolical

Illuminati were suppressed by the Bavarian government in 1785. His sect went underground, and with the help of the Rothschilds of Frankfurt they took over the French Masonic Grand Orient and surfaced in the French Revolution. The executioners who manned the guillotines were from this diabolical Illuminati sect, and Mirabeau and Robespierre were Illuminati. There were cells of republican freethinkers called Illuminati in Italy: in Milan, Bologna, Rome and Naples. Their combination of republicanism and murder guided Napoleon. Later on, they financed Karl Marx and eventually the Russian Revolution under Kerensky, when the wealth of the Russian Tsars passed into their hands.

In Britain there had been another secret society which eventually teamed up with the heretical, Luciferian Illuminati. It seems to have begun with Bacon, and to have been concerned with his 'new world' vision of a new Atlantis. It seems to have drawn on the occult researches of John Dee, and to have been linked with the new secret service of Walsingham and with Elizabeth I (whom one royal tradition describes as having been a man, always wearing a wig to cover her bald head). Marlowe, one of Walsingham's spies, caught the occultist background to the age in his *Dr Faustus*, and there are many references to witchcraft in Shakespeare.

This secret society, which was linked with Walsingham's, had dealings with Britain's enemies: first, with Spain during the time of the Spanish Armada, when it too opposed the Catholic Spanish Habsburg Alumbrado Light with Dee's occultist Neoplatonist-Kabbalist and probably Luciferian light; and later, in the 17th century, with the Netherlands; in the 18th century with France and in the 20th century with Germany. At all times, when Britain was publicly at war with a nation, the secret society was in touch with the enemy. At some time, probably around the end of the Napoleonic wars and the Congress of Vienna, it merged with the German-Italian Masonic Illuminati, and the House of Rothschild played a key role in this new secret alliance.

Some time after the 1780s, the Alumbrados, Rosicrucians and Bavarian Illuminati were woven together into the Committee of 300, which began soon after the American war of 1812. The Committee of 300 has always controlled the US, and still does, and is a secret society. It embodies the inheritors of Illuminism, both its original mystical form (the Alumbrados and Habsburg Light) and its heretical, diabolical form – the Satanistic Illuminati (now known as Moriah Conquering Wind), the cults of Dionysus and Isis, Catharism and Bogomilism. There are 300 organizations behind the Committee, who think of themselves as 'Olympians' as their God is Lucifer and they are higher than the Christian God. The Committee was modelled on the British East India Company, which itself came out of the Venetian slave trade, and its programme is based on Malthus, whose population control was favoured by the British East India Company. The Malthusian programme the Committee have operated since 1980 is known as 'Global 2000' – a 'Global 2000 Report' was written for the Committee by Cyrus Vance (later a 'Peacekeeper' in Bosnia) and accepted by President Carter – and the target is to reduce the world's population from rising six billion to under four billion by 2000, a reduction of two billion or a third of humankind by encouraging local wars, famines and disease. The Bosnian war, the African famines and AIDS all have to be seen as part of their plan to kill 'useless eaters' ('Global 2000 Report').

The Committee now includes, *ex officio*, the head of the Habsburg family, whose ancestors knew the original mystical Illuminati; the British monarch, whose predecessor Elizabeth I knew the occultism of Dee; and heirs of the diabolical Illuminati, such as Moriah Conquering Wind. The Committee includes the Venetian and Black Nobility families of Europe (the families that derived their titles from the Papacy rather than the temporal state); the English and Scottish families that surround the British Monarchy; the other royal families of Europe, including the Danish, Norwegian and Dutch royal families; the American Eastern Liberal establishment families (families ranked in a hierarchy according to their involvement in Freemasonry and the Order of Skull and Bones); and the organizations which act as the Committee's offshoots, such as the Royal Institute for International Affairs, the Bilderberg Group, the Trilateral Commission and the Club of Rome (which has played a crucial role in the policies of our time).

It seems likely that this Committee, which draws on hundreds of institutions, has within it a mini-committee of nine, which are mirrored in Masonic groups such as the Nine Unknown Men. In historical terms the nine are likely to include a representative from Britain, the Netherlands (Prince Bernhard), Germany, Spain, Italy, the Vatican, France, Russia and America. (Japan seems to have associate status and membership of the Trilateral Commission).

A faction within the Committee of 300 that subscribes to Luciferian ideas apparently plans to make a 'sacrifice' as part of the Global 2000 population control programme. Leaks say that there will be a sacrifice of Sefardic Jews in Israel to release their energy into space (an occultist notion many will find hard to believe).

The Committee have worked for a world government for nearly 200 years. Such a world government would reunite Britain and the US, restoring the position of the 1780s. Having attempted to bring about a world government through Napoleon, Stalin and Hitler, the Committee is determined to bring in a New World Order by the year 2000. This New World Order may begin sooner than that. There are disturbing and probably incredible reports of what may happen to people who resist. Some suggest they will be subjected to mind-control. (If bombarded by microwaves of 425 megacycles, human beings lose the power to resist and become like zombies, sleep-walking slaves who will do what they are told.) Some suggest there will be military actions. In many developed countries, bridges and motorways have been strengthened to take tanks, and ring roads (such as the M25 round London) have been built round key cities to facilitate a military stranglehold. It is being said that once the invasion has taken place, there will be a world financial crisis as money will be abolished for several weeks and everyone will be required to register for work. It is said that farms will be requisitioned, and that government plans for coping with looters already exist; that Britain (for one) has been split into zones. Some suggest that Cambodia was a model for what may follow: that millions of people will be turned out of the cities into the countryside, that they will be prevented from returning by the military presence round the cities and the cameras, and that executioners will take a cull and the survivors will be set to work.

If such stories are true, then the Committee of 300 are under the control of a neo-Fascist few whose Nazi policies will dwarf the Holocaust. A world government (and Committee) that stops wars and famines and diseases can only be good for the world; a world government (and Committee) that is already preparing concentration camps and proposing to kill two billion people can only be a disaster for the world.

ACKNOWLEDGEMENTS

The *One and the Many* is based on articles and lectures I gave between 1993 and 1998. These pieces came after *The Universe and the Light* and reflect my thinking during these five years. The concerns and themes that weave in and out of them were addressed to different audiences.

I have made some changes where there was overlapping. 'Revolution: Reclaiming the Palace of Metaphysics' was written for a national newspaper. 'Living in a Universe of Fire' appeared in *Caduceus*, issue 21, 1993. 'Reductionist Science and Philosophy – and the Fire' was written at the request of *Resurgence*, and 'The Light that Became the Universe' for the *Vintage Times*. 'The Metaphysical Universe and the Metaphysical Revolution' appeared in the *Radionic Quarterly*, summer 1993. 'Towards a Universalist Theory of Everything' was an address to the College of Psychic Studies on 19 October 1993. 'A New Mystic and Philosophical Universalism' began as an address to the Quaker Universalist Group's conference in Birmingham on 18 April 1993, and a long extract appeared in the Group's journal, *Universalist*, September 1993. 'What is Universalism?' was written for the Universalist Philosophy Group. 'A Philosophy of Fire' appeared in *Resurgence*, November/December 1993.

'Intuitionist Universalism and the Fire Behind the Universe' was a public address at a day's event put on by the Universalist Philosophy Group under the banner, 'Universalism and the New Metaphysics' on 15 October 1994. 'The Fire or Light as Common Ground for a Universal or World-Wide Civilization and Religion' was an address given to the Alister Hardy Society in Kensington Square on 18 May 1995. 'Revolution in Thought and Culture' was a public address given at the Jubilee Hall, Aldeburgh on 3 October 1997. 'In the Garden of the One' was an address I gave to the Cambridge Arts Visits Group at the Garden House Hotel, Cambridge on 28 January 1998.

Readers of my poetic epic, *Overlord*, which I began in October 1994, will relate some of the poetic passages in that work to these pieces.

Nicholas Hagger